CONTENTS

Trainers assist Buffalo Bills tight end Kevin Everett after he suffered a severe injury to his spine during the second half of a Bills game against the Denver Broncos. Quick response and advanced knowledge of spinal injuries and treatment techniques by the Bills' medical staff made it possible for Everett to walk again.

Thirty-one minutes into an exhibition game between the women's U.S. soccer team and Brazil, forward Abby Wambach collided violently with a defender from the Brazilian team while attempting to take a shot on goal. Wambach tumbled into the air and fell onto the field. She immediately signaled to the sideline for help. The U.S. team's medical staff ran onto the field. They assessed her injuries—a broken tibula and fibula—and immobilized her leg. They carried her off the field on a stretcher and took her to a hospital for X-rays. After surgery and months of physical therapy, Wambach returned to the soccer field and was instrumental in leading the U.S. team to the 2011 World Cup finals.

In 2007, Buffalo Bills tight end Kevin Everett sustained a life-threatening spinal cord injury while trying to make a tackle during the Bills' season-opening football game against the Denver Broncos. He lay paralyzed on the field as the Bills' medical staff tended to him. In the ambulance on the way to the hospital, orthopedic surgeon Andrew Cappuccino, who works for the Bills as a medical consultant specializing in spinal surgeries, began cold therapy. This cutting-edge technique is used to chill the body from the inside. Cappuccino's advanced knowledge of spinal injuries was responsible for Everett's ability to move his arms and legs just days later. Although Everett never returned to the football field, he is now able to walk—a positive outcome that is due to the diligence and expertise of Cappuccino and the team's medical staff.

The sport of golf is often referred to as a mental game. No one knows this better than Dr. Patrick Cohn, a golf psychology expert and author of *The Golfer's Mental Edge*. Cohn teaches mental skills and sports psychology techniques to amateur and professional golfers as a way to help them improve their game. He works with the golfers to help them remove the mental barriers that keep them from playing well. He also helps athletes build confidence so that they perform at their best. Cohn is a leader in the field of sports psychology, a branch of sports medicine that is becoming increasingly important within the sports industry.

These are just three examples of how important sports fitness and medicine professionals are to athletes. From assessing injuries during games and rehabilitating injured athletes so that they can return to play, to improving the mental toughness that participants need to compete at the highest levels of their sport, sports fitness and medicine professionals play a crucial role in the lives and careers of athletes. These professionals help keep athletes healthy, both physically and mentally, and assist them in achieving and maintaining peak performance.

The field of sports medicine and fitness is large. Jobs within it vary from sports medicine physicians, athletic trainers, personal trainers, and sports psychologists, to physical therapists, strength and conditioning coaches, nutritionists, and massage therapists. There is a wide range of places to work, from professional sports organizations to high schools, and the jobs can vary from highly paid jobs to volunteer opportunities. The field is as competitive as it is exciting and rewarding.

Chapter 1

THE FIELD OF DREAMS: SPORTS FITNESS AND MEDICINE

Peyton Manning, the Super Bowl–winning quarterback for the Indianapolis Colts and four-time National Football League (NFL) Most Valuable Player (MVP), learned firsthand how valuable sports fitness and medicine professionals are to a team. In the spring of 2011, Manning underwent surgery to repair a bulging disc in his neck. The surgery took place during the NFL lockout, a time when players and team owners were negotiating a new labor contract and most league activities were suspended. Because of the lockout, players were not allowed to practice, seek the medical attention of anyone associated with the team, or use any of the team's facilities. Normally, an athlete's care is overseen, even in the off-season, by the team's medical staff. In the fall, just before the 2011 season began, Manning underwent a second surgery on his neck after concluding that he was not recovering properly from the earlier one. In interviews, he cited the lockout and his inability to rehabilitate with the team's medical staff as a major reason for his slow recovery from the first surgery and subsequent setback.

Manning saw just how important sports medicine is to an athlete's overall health and to keeping a player at the top of his or her game. Athletes need more than coaches to succeed. They need the support of sports fitness and medicine professionals who help them train properly, maintain healthy eating habits, and prevent injury. They also assess and diagnose injuries when they happen and create a plan

Injured Indianapolis Colts quarterback Peyton Manning watches from the sidelines as his team plays a pre-season game. Manning had surgery to repair a bulging disc in his neck.

for rebuilding strength and recovering from an injury so that athletes can return to play as quickly as possible. Partly because of Manning's inability to work with his usual team of sports fitness and medicine professionals, his recovery stalled and a second surgery was needed. As a result, he missed the entire 2011 season.

Many people think of professional sports teams when they think of sports fitness and medicine professionals. While some of the most visible jobs are with professional, semipro, and college sports teams (who hasn't seen a trainer rush onto the field, court, or ice during competitive play to tend to an athlete who has been injured?), those are just a few of the ways that sports fitness and medicine professionals are employed. Sports medicine professionals can also be found at colleges and universities, health care clinics, health clubs and gyms, and even community centers. It's a broad field that includes a wide range of jobs.

Indeed, sports medicine is one of the fastest-growing areas of health care. Sports medicine professionals help everyone from professional athletes to everyday people who enjoy working out, playing pickup games with friends, or just being physically active.

WHAT IS SPORTS MEDICINE?

Sports medicine is a broad field that focuses on the care, treatment, and prevention of sports-related injuries. There are a number of areas of specialization—from team physicians and athletic trainers who assess, diagnose, and treat injuries, to nutritionists who design healthy menus and sports psychologists who help athletes overcome the mental barriers to performance. The field encompasses many specialties, including clinical medicine, exercise physiology, orthopedics, kinesiology, physical therapy, athletic training, massage therapy, sports nutrition, psychology, and sports medical research. Each career path has its own set of responsibilities, educational requirements, rewards, and challenges.

Sports fitness and medicine professionals work in a variety of environments, including the great outdoors. Two ski patrol medics assist a skier who has injured a leg on the slopes.

The field of sports medicine is growing like never before. This is due to the increasing importance of athletics, fitness, and health in our daily lives. The professional sports industry contributes billions of dollars to the economy. Also, more and more ordinary people are playing sports and working out. So sports medicine professionals are needed to treat the injuries that will inevitably occur. They must also educate athletes—professionals and amateurs alike—on how to prevent these injuries from happening in the first place.

According to reports, the most common injuries treated in emergency rooms are the consequence of sports-related activities. Five sports—cycling, basketball, baseball, running, and skiing—account for more than 215,000 injuries each year in the U.S. alone.

CAREERS IN SPORTS FITNESS AND MEDICINE

There are so many choices for someone who is interested in working in sports medicine. Breaking into the field can begin as early as high school. Educational requirements can vary as widely as the number of career options that exist.

For many, a career in sports fitness and medicine is a combination of two passions: a love of sports and a passion for healing the human body and/or seeing an athlete

MASSAGE THERAPY HELPS MICHAEL PHELPS AT THE OLYMPICS

Michael Phelps, the winner of fourteen gold medals and two bronze medals at three different Olympics, drew a lot of attention during the 2008 Beijing Olympic Games. Poolside, Phelps was often seen getting a massage immediately after his races. Having a massage therapist at the pool helped the swimmer prepare his body before a race and speed his recovery afterward.

In Beijing, Phelps was competing for an unprecedented eight gold medals in one Olympics. As a result, his swim schedule was intensive. On any given day, he was often competing twice. Sometimes Phelps would swim a qualifying race in one event in the morning and swim the finals of a second event in the afternoon. Massage therapy played a key role in helping Phelps prepare for the demands of this schedule. With races so close together, his muscles needed to recover quickly so that he could be at the top of his game the next time he swam.

As Phelps helped demonstrate, massage is part of most athletes' training regimens and recovery strategies. It is one of the best ways to help muscles bounce back after intensive workouts or competitions. The 2008 Olympic Games were perhaps the first time a massage therapist was so prominently visible on the sidelines of a competition. When Phelps went on to win eight gold medals in Beijing, his overwhelming success raised the profile of the massage therapy profession and drew attention to the enormous benefits it offers to athletes.

perform to his or her full potential. There are numerous career paths, each one requiring a different level of education. Some require certifications, while others require advanced degrees. So many choices means that, while the range in salary also varies, there is sure to be a career path that meets your interests and career goals.

THE IMPORTANCE OF SPORTS MEDICINE AND FITNESS

The role that sports fitness and medicine professionals play has grown in significance as more and more people engage in sports and fitness activities. Sports fitness and medicine professionals are well-trained individuals who contribute greatly to amateur athletic programs and professional sports organizations. For college and professional teams, there is a lot at stake—including millions of dollars—when an athlete gets injured. Preventing injuries is important, and treating them quickly when they occur is vital to getting an athlete back into top shape.

Sports medicine is not restricted to physicians who specialize in sports-related injuries. The field has grown to include specialists who cover a wide range of areas. As more research is conducted on the impact of physical activity on the human body, new career paths have popped up that focus on sports. Some of these include:

TEN HOT SPORTS MEDICINE TRENDS

The *Journal of the American College of Sports Medicine* has named ten trends in sports medicine:

1. **Educated and Experienced Sports Medicine Professionals:** In the past, only a little experience was all one needed to get a job in sports medicine. But now, as this field grows in both need and popularity, professionals are obtaining formal education, certifications, and licensures for nearly all career paths.

2. **Focus on Childhood Obesity:** More wellness and fitness programs are now available to help combat the nation's growing epidemic of childhood obesity.

3. **Personal Training:** Having a personal trainer was once a luxury that only the wealthy enjoyed. Today, with the proliferation of top-notch fitness facilities and certification programs, there has been a significant increase in the number of qualified personal trainers offering their services. A far larger segment of the population can now afford to hire one of these fitness experts.

4. **Increased Emphasis on Strength Training:** Aerobic exercise (running, walking, swimming, biking) used to be the focus for those wishing to get back into shape. But for overall fitness and health, strength training is key. It builds muscle and burns fat more effectively than aerobic exercise alone. It is also universally recognized as one of the best ways to maintain health as we age.

5. **Core Training:** The midsection of our bodies—the muscles that make up our abdomen—is referred to

as our core. Strengthening these muscles is a great way to prevent injury and maintain better health.

6. **Fitness for Older Adults:** Staying healthy as we age is important. Strength and fitness training can help older adults better perform daily tasks, and being in good shape can help ward off illness and disease.

7. **Balance Ball Training and Pilates:** Balance ball training is comprised of exercises performed while sitting, standing, or lying on a stability ball. These exercises have been proven to improve a person's core strength and balance. Pilates is a yoga-type exercise that focuses on flexibility, posture, and strength.

8. **Sports Specific Training:** Athletes are incorporating training routines specifically tailored to a particular sport as part of their overall training programs. These can include certain arm exercises for tennis players and baseball pitchers, leg conditioning for runners and soccer players, flexibility and strength routines for gymnasts, and endurance training for hockey and basketball players.

9. **Group Personal Training:** Groups of individuals are hiring personal trainers to design classes for at-home fitness. This group-style program helps each individual get personalized attention while cutting down on the costs of a personal trainer.

10. **Wellness Coaching:** Wellness coaches advise clients on how to live a healthier life through

exercise programs, nutri-
tion, stress reduction, and making better lifestyle choices, like quit-
ting smoking. Many companies are hiring
wellness coaches to help keep employees healthy.

- Nutritionist: A nutritionist is someone who plans meals in accordance with medical, nutritional, and other needs. A sports nutritionist might plan a high-energy menu for a baseball franchise or create personalized menus for athletes who have particular dietary or health goals. In general, a bachelor's degree is required for entry into the field. Degree programs in one of the following areas are most popular: dietetics, food and nutrition, and food service management. In addition, many states require licensure or certification.

- Chiropractor: A chiropractor adjusts imbalances in a person's posture or spine using manipulation, massage, and ultrasound therapy. A four-year advanced degree in chiropractic medicine is required and is completed after one earns a bachelor's degree.

- Exercise physiology: An exercise physiologist studies an athlete's physiological response to physical activity and then tries to improve the athlete's performance. At a minimum, one needs an undergraduate degree. While not required, earning a certification in the field can improve job prospects.

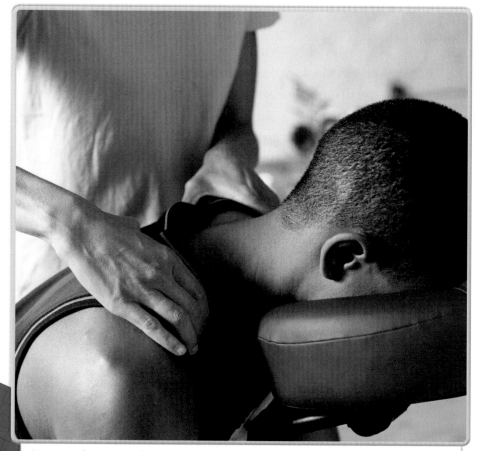

Massage therapy can help an athlete loosen his or her muscles before competition, treat an injury by increasing blood circulation, or assist in muscle recovery after a hard workout.

- Massage therapist: Massage therapists press, rub, and otherwise manipulate the muscles and other soft tissues of the body to alleviate pain and increase blood circulation. For athletes, massage can help muscles recover faster from grueling workouts or strenuous competition.

Every athlete knows the potential for injury is present each time he or she works out or competes. Athletes never know when they may suddenly twist an ankle, break a bone, strain a muscle, or tear a ligament. A well-trained medical team not only helps prevent injuries from happening but also can immediately treat an athlete when an injury does occur. Sometimes this quick response is the difference between missing a few days of practice or missing an entire season. Athletes also know that proper nutrition and mental toughness are crucial for their success. Sports fitness and medicine professionals cover all of these areas, and the right team of medical experts can make all the difference in one's quest for athletic success and good health.

Chapter 2

BECOMING A SPORTS FITNESS AND MEDICINE PROFESSIONAL

Sports fitness and medicine is an exciting and rewarding field. Many young people want to know how to obtain the education and background necessary to score one of these amazing jobs and begin working as soon as possible. Attending college and earning a degree is a necessity for success in the field. However, with such a wide range of jobs available, the amount of higher education required can vary depending on which job you find most interesting.

For example, one would need to complete a bachelor's degree, attend medical school, and complete internships and residencies before seeking out a position as a team physician. At a minimum, athletic trainers need a bachelor's degree in a sports-related field. They must also pass a national certification exam and become licensed in the state in which they wish to work. A nutritionist, on the other hand, may need only a two-year degree in nutrition.

Personal trainers need no college degree, and certifications in training are optional though advisable. With so many job options available in the field of sports medicine and fitness, there are many different routes to take depending on which specific career interests you most.

GETTING STARTED

Most high school students begin to think about future careers in the ninth and tenth grade, when they consider what subjects they like, what particular skills they have, and how they might apply these skills and interests to a job. In their junior or senior year, students often get more serious about examining the paths they need to pursue in order to be accepted into the college programs of their choice and successfully enter the professional field that interests them.

For those interested in sports fitness and medicine, career training can begin as early as high school. Students can volunteer on high school or local college sports teams as an assistant to a trainer or coach. There's no better way to learn about a job than to see exactly what kind of work the field's professionals actually perform each day. This type of experience gives interested students an inside look at how a sports team functions, what each person on the team's staff does, and whether the duties and work environment suit their interests and abilities.

Another option for high school students interested in investigating sports medicine and fitness is to first gain hands-on experience in the medical field. This allows them to confirm that treating and curing the ill is something they have an aptitude for and a genuine interest in. Becoming a volunteer for the local fire department, hospital, or emergency medical response team is an excellent way to observe how medical staff respond to patients requiring help. It will test one's skills and suitability for the demands of the work.

Once a student knows which sports fitness and medicine career path he or she wants to pursue, the next step

Gaining experience in the medical field is one way of learning if the sports fitness and medicine field is for you. Volunteering with your local fire department, hospital, or ambulance corps gives you hands-on experience working with patients and medical professionals.

is to begin looking at the requirements of each job, which college programs and majors offer the best preparation, and what additional credentials, such as certifications or licensures, are needed.

WHAT WILL I STUDY?

Many colleges look for well-rounded applicants with good grades in science, math, writing, and the liberal arts. The choice of which major to pursue hinges on what career field you hope to enter upon graduation. The most common undergraduate majors for careers in sports fitness and medicine include:

- **Health and exercise science**. The study of the human body and physical activity, with the goal of helping athletes better their performance on the field or improve their level of fitness.

- **Kinesiology**. Sometimes called human kinetics, kinesiology is the scientific study of human movement. Kinesiology majors study how the human body moves, why it moves the way it does, what happens to our bodies when they are in motion, and how they respond to exercise and rehabilitation when we are injured.

- **Sports medicine**. The understanding, prevention, and rehabilitation of injuries

Sports fitness and medicine professionals work with athletes of all ages and guide them on training techniques, physical fitness, preventing injuries, treating injuries, and improving their level of fitness.

brought on by physical activity. Sports medicine programs include course work in injury prevention, the fundamentals of motor skills, human physiology, athletic training, biomechanics, and nutrition and performance.

- **Athletic training**. The course work in this program educates students on preventing, recognizing, managing, and rehabilitating injuries that result from physical activity.

- **Physical education**. This popular major often leads to students becoming physical education teachers at the elementary or secondary levels. But this program of study can also lead to jobs in sports medicine and fitness since both fields share course work in understanding muscular strength, cardiovascular conditioning, and athletic endurance.

Beyond a degree program, there are certifications and licensures that may be needed, depending on which career path you choose to pursue. Athletic trainers are required to be licensed in most states. They must meet education and clinical experience requirements before they can sit for a national certification exam. Team physicians are medical doctors. As such, they must complete a bachelor's degree, attend medical school, and pass medical board tests before they can practice medicine. A massage therapist attends a training program and, depending on the state in which he or she practices, must have national or state certification. Each career area within the sports fitness and medicine field has its own requirements, and these are discussed in full in the following chapters.

GAINING EXPERIENCE

Breaking into the sports fitness and medicine field requires experience, which can be gained through internships, graduate assistantships, or sports medicine fellowships, either during or just after the completion of one's educa-

As part of your education and training, gaining experience through an internship is a great way to learn what sports fitness professionals do on a daily basis. It's also the best way to meet professionals in the field who can help advise you on your career aspirations.

tion. These programs provide hands-on experience that can boost your résumé and help gain you a full-time job.

Internships are often unpaid opportunities for students to work alongside professionals in a given field. Many college students already enrolled in a sports fitness or medicine program seek out internships as part of their education. Students might observe an athletic trainer, sports psychologist, physical therapist, strength and conditioning coach, nutritionist, or massage therapist at work, and this will help them better understand what the jobs entail, what their responsibilities are, how these professionals got their jobs, and exactly what they do on a day-to-day basis. Internships are a great way to get noticed by an employer and gain real-world work experience while still in college.

Graduate assistantships are positions offered to students who are completing advanced degrees in graduate school. These positions are offered by and support the efforts of an office or department at the college or university where the student is enrolled and can provide valuable work experience. Assistantships for students pursuing master's degrees in sports fitness and medicine might include positions with the college's athletic department or with the medical staff of one of the school's sports teams. Graduate assistants can gain a great deal of practical, hands-on experience through these assignments. Their day-to-day responsibilities can include traveling with the team and

Interning or getting a job with a college sports team offers a valuable opportunity to learn from athletic trainers, strength and conditioning coaches, physical therapists, and even head coaches while they work on the field during games.

conducting drug testing and educational programs. Under the supervision of the team physician, physical therapist, or athletic trainer, they may assist in the actual treatment of athletes. Often times, graduate assistants are also responsible for documenting medical evaluations and treatments completed by athletes. Many also help operate and maintain the athletic facilities.

The most comprehensive way to gain hands-on professional experience is through a sports medicine fellowship. A fellowship is a program designed to train individuals in the management of problems experienced

FIVE WAYS TO GET A JOB IN SPORTS MEDICINE

Are you eager to get a job in sports medicine? Here are five ways to get your foot in the door and gain the experience you need to land the job you want:

1. **Choose a Specialty:** The field of sports medicine and fitness is large and diverse and includes a wide range of career paths. But to gain a job in the field, you must select one area as your specialty. After researching the different disciplines, choose one and dedicate yourself to completing the requirements you need to make yourself competitive in that particular area. Select the right major in college, work toward the certifications or licenses you may need, and get practical experience through internships and volunteering.

2. **Get an Education:** After selecting which field you want to pursue, get the education you need to be successful. A career as a sports physician, sports psychologist, or physical therapist requires a college education and graduate school. Massage therapists and strength and conditioning coaches often need experience and certifications to get started. Each job's educational requirements vary, so do some research before selecting a program.

3. **Get Experience:** The best way to gain experience is to volunteer or complete an internship in your field of interest. These opportunities give you hands-on experience as you learn from and work alongside professionals in sports medicine. As an added benefit, you get to see firsthand what a professional in your field does each day, giving you the chance to determine if that career path best meets your skills and interests.

4. Learn from the Best: Volunteering and internships not only give you experience, they also introduce you to working professionals in the field. Seek out the best people in your career field to learn from. Observe them at work, ask questions, read any articles they have written, and attend training sessions they offer.

5. Set Yourself Apart: Combine your education and experience to become an expert in your field. If your passion is football, work on learning the ins and outs of sports medicine as it relates to football-related injuries. Maybe you are interested in helping high school athletes learn more about how nutrition can improve their performance. Developing a talent in a particular area can draw attention to yourself and make you a valued asset to a team or employer.

by athletes and those who exercise. Fellowships offer experience in clinical care, athletic department support, education, and research. They are difficult to obtain and often require applicants to have strong educational backgrounds and some level of experience. Once obtained, however, they can lead to exciting jobs and help to further advance one's career.

The American Medical Society for Sports Medicine and the American Orthopaedic Society for Sports Medicine both offer sports medicine fellowships. These programs require applicants to have completed medical school before they apply. Some universities, such as the University of Wisconsin at Madison, offer fellowships through which applicants can gain experience working with the school's Division I sports teams.

FINDING A JOB

The Internet has made the process of seeking a job in the sports fitness and medicine field far easier than it once was. Sports teams, colleges and universities, athletic training facilities, and other places that employ professionals in sports fitness and medicine now post job openings and accept résumés and applications on their Web sites. There are also professional organizations that post job listings related to this career field. In addition, certain search engines concentrate on locating jobs within the sports fitness and medicine industry.

To begin an online job search, visit some of the search engines devoted specifically to sports fitness and medicine or whose search parameters can be narrowed to focus only on this field. The leading job search engines are:

- **Indeed.com**. A search engine that finds a variety of job postings from all over the Internet.

- **SimplyHired.com**. This site's main page allows you to search job boards, classified ads, job postings on sites like Craigslist, and company job postings. Searching by keyword and location can help narrow the search results.

- **Monster.com**. One of the first online job search sites, Monster.com allows you to search jobs, post your résumé, research employer information, network with professionals in the field, create job alerts, and use resources like résumé-writing techniques and interviewing tips.

- **NSCA Jobs Boards**. The career resource Web site of the National Strength and Conditioning Association, the site offers job postings and networking opportunities in the health and fitness industry. You need to join, but members can upload resumes to jobs they want to apply for.

- **ACSM Job Center**. The Web site of the American College of Sports Medicine, this site targets career opportunities in sports medicine for nurses, physicians, and physician assistants.

The best way to locate a job on any search engine is to target your search using keywords associated with the

The American College of Sports Medicine's Web site (www.acsm.org) features a career services page that highlights internships, job openings, and career opportunities in sports medicine for nutritionists, nurses, physical therapists, physicians, and physician assistants.

field of sports medicine. Use key word search terms like "sports medicine," "strength coach," "health or fitness," "personal trainer," "sports specialist," "sports rehabilitation," or "sports performance." You can also search using a job title or college major.

Chapter 3

TEAM PHYSICIANS

When New York Yankees pitcher Phil Hughes began to experience a significant drop in the speed of his pitches during spring training, he turned to the Yankees' head physician for help. After working with a coach to try some different pitching techniques, it became clear that Hughes had a medical problem. Hughes told team physician Dr. Christopher Ahmad that he was feeling fatigue in his right arm and shoulder. Dr. Ahmad examined Hughes and recommended an MRI, along with tests to check the pitcher's blood circulation.

Like most professional sports team physicians, Dr. Ahmad is a specialist. He is an expert in injuries affecting the knees, shoulders, and elbows—some of the most common areas that experience injury among baseball players. After reviewing Hughes's test results, Dr. Ahmad was able to diagnose the pitcher's injury. He then recommended a treatment and rehabilitation plan to get Hughes's arm and

Phil Hughes, a pitcher for the New York Yankees, was experiencing problems with the speed of his pitches and had some soreness in his shoulder. Dr. Christopher Ahmad, the team's physician, examined the pitcher's arm and shoulder and ordered tests. After getting treatment, Hughes was back on the pitcher's mound.

shoulder strong enough again for the all-star pitcher to return to play.

WHAT IS A TEAM PHYSICIAN?

Professional and college athletes spend the majority of their daily life training or competing in their sport. Because of this, they put themselves at risk for injury due to the sheer amount of time they spend working out, training, and practicing. When they do get hurt, these athletes need the best doctors and medical care available. It's the job of the sports team physician to oversee their medical care so that they can return to competition as quickly as possible.

Most team physicians are in charge of coordinating the medical staff and medical services for a sports team. A sports doctor is a fully qualified medical doctor who has chosen to focus on sports medicine as his or her specialty. Team physicians also provide for the well-being of individual athletes.

As doctors, they must be knowledgeable about medical conditions encountered while playing sports. They must be able to work together with other members of the team's medical staff (such as athletic trainers, nutritionists, and physical therapists). They coordinate various treatments for an athlete. Doctors must be able to assume responsibility for making medical decisions that affect

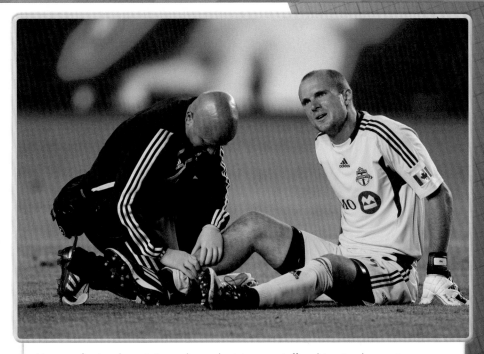

Many professional sports teams have physicians on staff and in attendance at games. When injuries occur, physicians can respond immediately. This was the case with Stefan Frei, the goalkeeper for Toronto FC, who injured his shin during a soccer game.

the athlete's participation in team activities while healthy or when returning from an injury. When an athlete is injured, it's the team doctor, not the team's coach, who decides when the athlete is physically ready to return to competition.

Because they are in charge of an athlete's health, team physicians have a wide range of duties. Among the biggest responsibilities is managing each athlete's medical condition. This can involve a range of activities. Team physicians coordinate the screening, examination, and evaluation of an athlete before he or she begins practice for the season. They order tests and exams as needed to assess injuries. They manage the assessment of injuries on the field. Team physicians coordinate rehabilitation among the team's medical staff. They conduct exams to ensure an athlete has completed treatment and is ready to return to competitive play. They also manage and coordinate all of the team's medical staff.

A team physician works with individual athletes, the coaching staff, the team's management, and even outside medical staff, who may be consulted on injuries that are uncommon or rare.

EDUCATIONAL REQUIREMENTS

Becoming a physician is a lengthy process that requires dedication. The education requirements include a bachelor's degree, medical school, and advanced medical training. Team physicians are required to have an advanced degree, such as an MD (doctor of medicine) or DO (doctor of osteopathic medicine). In addition to medical school course work, team physicians also need experience or education in cardiac rehabilitation, general radiology, orthopedic surgical techniques, and respiratory rehabilitation. These are all important areas of specialization related to sports and physical activity.

All doctors begin their education with a bachelor's degree. Students can choose to major in one of the sciences, such as biology, biotechnology, chemistry, or physics. At this point they are referred to as premed students. As undergraduates, premed students can take elective courses in areas related to sports medicine to gain an understanding of the field. Courses in physical education, kinesiology, and strength and conditioning can provide some initial knowledge of the types of issues team physicians will encounter on the job. Students may also choose a minor, which is a select group of courses that provides a secondary area of expertise outside a student's major. Minors in areas such as exercise science, sports management,

Physicians spend four years in medical school, followed by a residency at a hospital, where they gain hands-on experience examining, diagnosing, and treating patients.

or sports psychology offer a good foundation for further study in one of those fields and a more well-rounded pre-med education.

Medical school follows the bachelor's degree and features four years of intensive study. During this time, students learn about biochemistry, genetics, pharmacology, anatomy, and physiology, among other areas. After completing their course work, students begin clinical rotations. During rotations, they spend several weeks engaging in hands-on learning in areas such as internal medicine, general surgery, pediatrics, psychiatry, obstetrics and gynecology, family medicine, and others. After graduating from medical school, new doctors are not yet ready to practice medicine. They are required to complete a residency first.

A medical residency consists of three to seven years of professional training under the supervision of senior physicians who are medical educators. The length of residency training varies depending on the specialty a doctor chooses. For example, family practice, internal medicine, and pediatrics require three years of residency, while general surgery requires five years. Many sports physicians choose to complete a residency in orthopedics. This is an area of medicine that focuses on the musculoskeletal system and the ability of our muscles and skeletal systems to work together to create motion.

Sometimes a sports physician will also have completed a fellowship, which provides an additional one to three years of training in a subspecialty area of medicine. A fellowship is an option for doctors who want to become highly specialized in a particular field, such as sports medicine. There are a number of fellowships available in sports medicine. These offer concentrated experience in the prevention, treatment, and care of injuries caused by athletic training and competition.

After completing undergraduate, medical school, and advanced medical education, a physician must obtain a license to practice medicine from the state in which he or she decides to practice. Each state has its own educa-

As part of their residency, physicians work with a number of different types of doctors and gain experience in a wide variety of medical fields, including pediatrics, internal medicine, orthopedics, rehabilitation, and emergency medicine.

SPORTS MEDICINE SPECIALIZATIONS

A sports team physician may choose to pursue a specialization in a particular field of medicine related to sports and sports injury. Fields that enhance a physician's knowledge of the treatment and care of sports-related injuries include:

- **Emergency Medicine:** A physician who specializes in emergency medicine focuses on the immediate decision-making and action necessary to treat a patient during an emergency situation. Emergency medicine includes the evaluation, diagnosis, stabilization, and care of a patient immediately after an injury occurs. In sports, particularly those in which direct contact with another athlete can cause serious injury (such as football and hockey), the treatment of an injury moments after it happens can mean the difference between a few months of rehabilitation and the end of an athlete's sports career, lifelong debility, or even death.

- **Orthopedic Medicine:** This is the evaluation and treatment of musculoskeletal problems. Athletes who have injured their shoulders, elbows, or knees have orthopedic surgery to fix and restore damage caused during physical activity. Orthopedic surgeons can specialize in a particular body part, such as the spine, hands, feet, knee, hip, shoulder, elbow, hand, or neck.

- **Rehabilitative Medicine:** This specialty focuses on the evaluation and treatment of athletes

with short- or long-
term physical injuries.
Some injuries to the spine,
neck, shoulder, or knee require
continual care to maintain a full range of
motion and to help restore strength. Rehabilitative medicine repairs and restores function
to an injured athlete.

tional requirements that must be fulfilled before one can sit for the certifying exam. A medical license is temporary. Doctors apply for the permanent license after completing a series of exams and completing a minimum number of years of advanced medical education.

Many doctors also choose to become board certified, which is an optional process. Specialty board certification establishes that a doctor is proficient and expert in a specialized area of medicine. Sports physicians often choose a specialty in emergency medicine, sports medicine, orthopedic sports medicine, or rehabilitative medicine.

Even after all these years of study and training, the education process never really ends for a physician. Doctors are required to complete a certain amount of continuing education each year to maintain their medical license. They must also stay on top of the latest in medical advances, techniques, and technologies. Ongoing medical education requirements can vary by state, by professional organization, and by a physician's employer.

WHERE WILL I WORK?

The most common places for sports doctors to work are with professional and college sports teams or in private practice. Some doctors, like Dr. Ahmad, the Yankees' team doctor, are also members of a large medical practice. Dr. Ahmad works for the Center for Shoulder, Elbow, and Sports Medicine, part of the Columbia University Medical Center in New York City. Through his position at the center, Dr. Ahmad is not only the head team physician for the Yankees, but he is also the team physician for the seventeen varsity teams at the City College of New York and for several high schools in Manhattan and New Jersey.

Teams may hire a sports physician who becomes a permanent member of their medical staff. Other times, physicians work as consultants for a sports team for a short period of time. In this case, they often treat a specific injury that falls within their area of specialization or to help educate athletes on diet, fitness, and injury prevention. Many times, a sports doctor works with only one team or organization and hones his or her knowledge of the injuries that occur most often in that particular sport.

While it is common for physicians to be employed at the amateur, college, semipro, and professional levels, finding employment in high school sports is rare. Most high schools do not employ team physicians. Instead, high schools often have a physician who volunteers his or

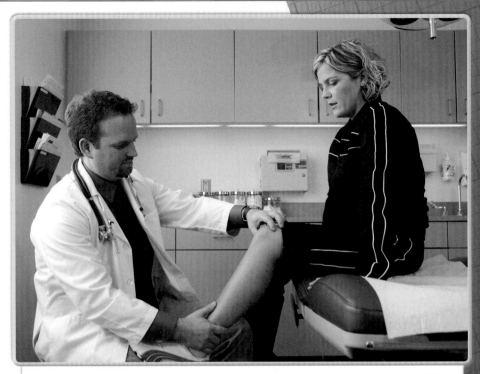

Sports physicians are employed in a wide variety of settings, from private clinics and hospitals to college and professional sports teams.

her time and consults with athletes and the coaching staff when an athlete is injured.

CAREER ADVANCEMENT

After becoming a doctor and gaining the experience necessary for a specialization in sports medicine, most sports physicians begin their careers in the field by working for a team. Career advancement can take many forms. For example, one may stay with a sports team and move up the ranks in responsibility until he or she becomes the

AN EMERGING CAREER FIELD: THE PHYSICIAN ASSISTANT

With more than seventy-three thousand physician assistants working in the United States, this emerging career field is growing by leaps and bounds. The field doesn't require medical school or the grueling internship that follows. So what is a physician assistant?

Physician assistants are health care professionals licensed to practice medicine under the supervision of a physician. They work under a doctor in any number of specialized areas of health care, such as family medicine, orthopedics, pediatrics, or emergency medicine.

With so many athletes to care for on professional sports teams, many team medical staffs employ physician assistants to support the team doctor. Working with a broad range of responsibilities, physician assistants keep athlete's medical histories up-to-date, conduct physical exams, order and interpret laboratory tests, and diagnose common injuries and illnesses. They also initiate treatment plans with other members of the medical team, counsel athletes to promote wellness and injury prevention, and apply casts and sutures when minor injuries occur.

head team physician. Other team doctors may eventually decide to open a private practice that treats sports-related injuries. Some team physicians decide to enter the business side of sports administration by getting involved in the team's finances, marketing, or management.

CAREER OUTLOOK

The field of sports medicine is thriving. According to the U.S. Bureau of Labor Statistics, employment for all physicians and surgeons is predicted to grow by 22 percent from 2008 to 2018. However, finding a job as a team physician will be difficult. There are a limited number of professional sports teams, so a limited number of these positions are available. While the field is competitive, there are many paths to success, from private practice and volunteering opportunities with high school teams, to research on treatments and their effectiveness. For current salary information for sports doctors, please refer to the Bureau of Labor Statistics Web site (www.bls.gov).

Chapter 4
ATHLETIC TRAINERS

One of the biggest "wow" moments for Leigh Weiss, a full-time athletic trainer with the New York Giants professional football team, is watching an athlete return to the field to do what he loves after weeks or months of post-injury rehabilitation.

Everyone sees the athletic trainers run onto the field when a player gets injured, but few know what these trainers do every day. Athletic trainers attend every practice and every game. They travel with the team as they monitor each player's health, provide general medical assistance, and assess injuries when they occur. For Weiss and other athletic trainers, the ultimate goal—and the most rewarding aspect of their job—is knowing that they played a major role in helping an athlete return to the field healthy, stronger, and ready to compete again.

Byron Hansen, a strength trainer for the New York Giants, oversees the workout of wide receiver Amani Toomer during a practice at Giants Stadium, in East Rutherford, New Jersey.

WHAT IS AN ATHLETIC TRAINER?

An athletic trainer is a medical professional who specializes in the day-to-day medical care of athletes. They assesses injuries, provide emergency treatment, and create rehabilitation plans. They also assist injured athletes in completing strengthening programs in order to enable them to return to peak performance. Athletic trainers often work alongside doctors when an athlete has been injured. After an injury is diagnosed and initial medical treatment is provided by a physician, the athletic trainer takes over the day-to-day responsibilities of medical care, therapy, and rehabilitation.

An athletic trainer is an important part of a team's medical staff. Their responsibilities include:

- Assessing injuries

- Initiating a treatment plan when injuries occur

- Designing and implementing rehabilitation plans that allow an athlete to regain the strength he or she may have lost while injured

- Teaching athletes proper exercise techniques to avoid injury

- Overseeing the purchasing of sports equipment as needed for training and rehabilitation

Athletic trainers work with athletes to boost their strength, physical conditioning, and workout performance. Here, a trainer works with a runner. The trainer will make suggestions as to how the runner can increase her speed and endurance.

Athletic trainers work with a wide range of athletes, from elite college and professional players to amateur, everyday athletes simply looking to boost their strength, conditioning, fitness, and workout performance.

Athletic trainers can be found working in a variety of places. This can include athletic training facilities, schools (K–12, private schools, colleges, universities), outpatient rehabilitation clinics, hospitals, physician offices, and professional sport organizations. At each of these places of employment, their responsibilities may vary. For example, an athletic trainer at a high school may work with the physical education teachers to create injury prevention programs for the school's sports team. Or, under the direction of a physician, he or she may help treat students who have been injured. For the professional athlete who has suffered an injury that prevents him or her from continuing to play, an athletic trainer may help create a strength and rehabilitation program. Trainers educate players on proper techniques in exercise to help them avoid injury. They also apply tape, bandages, and braces before practices and games. At the professional level, trainers also assist in scouting new players and monitoring off-season training programs.

EDUCATIONAL REQUIREMENTS

Becoming an athletic trainer requires higher education, formal training, and certification. Many athletic trainers obtain a bachelor of science degree in sports medicine, kinesiology, athletic training, physical education, or exercise science. These programs include courses that cover injury prevention, first aid, emergency care, injury assessment, biomechanics, human anatomy and physiology, therapeutic options for care, and wellness and nutrition.

While students are earning their bachelor's degree, part of their learning takes place outside the classroom, in clinical settings. This is where students gain hands-on experience working alongside athletic trainers or other medical personnel. A minimum of two years of clinical education is required. This can take place in settings such as hospitals, medical clinics, or with sports teams.

After completing both the bachelor's degree and the clinical experience, but before beginning work as an athletic trainer, students must receive certification as a certified athletic trainer by passing a test given by the Board of Certification. This is a national organization that certifies entry-level athletic trainers. You can earn the certified athletic trainer

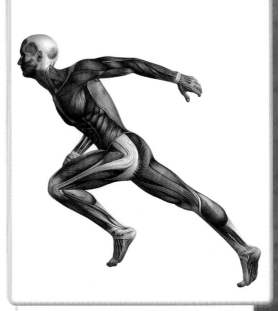

A significant part of the education for athletic trainers centers around physiology—an understanding of the human body and its muscles, ligaments, movements, and strength.

credential by meeting the board's educational requirements and passing the certification exam.

While a master's degree is not officially required, more than 70 percent of certified athletic trainers do have one, according to the National Athletic Trainers' Association (NATA). Those trainers seeking to expand their employment opportunities can earn a master's degree in athletic training, sports management, athletic administration, human movement, kinesiology, sport and exercise science, or sports physiology.

WHAT DO ATHLETIC TRAINERS DO IN THE OFF-SEASON?

So what do athletic trainers do in the off-season? Leigh Weiss, one of the New York Giants' athletic trainers, is often asked this very question. His response is that even though the football season is only five months long, there is a whole other side of an athletic trainer's job that begins immediately after the season is over. "As soon as the season ends, as an athletic training staff, we are working with our physicians to schedule any surgeries that our players may require or were put off during the season," he told AOLJobs.com. "We also are responsible for the rehabilitation after these operations, whether the player will be rehabbing with us or whether we need to find them a facility near their hometown."

NFL athletic trainers are also preparing for the NFL combine. This is a week-long, invitation-only event that gives college football players a chance to show off their skills to the recruiting staffs of the NFL teams. Trainers are also looking forward to the NFL draft, when college-level players are selected to join NFL teams. Athletic trainers gather medical information on all of the college prospects and help prepare reports for the teams' scouting departments on which players are physically, mentally, and emotionally ready for the demands of professional football. The combine and draft are followed by off-season strength and conditioning programs, physical exams of every player on the roster, mini training camps, and the full three- to four-week training camp that occurs over the summer. These lead up to regular practices and the first game of the season. The tireless work of athletic trainers is at the very heart of all of these activities.

WHERE WILL I WORK?

The job environment for an athletic trainer can vary. Many are employed by professional sports teams, colleges and universities with top athletic programs, and public and private high schools. You will also find athletic trainers working in hospitals, the military, and the performing arts. The various work settings include:

- **Secondary schools.** Many secondary schools are now recognizing the benefits of having an athletic trainer on staff to help prevent and care for student-athletes. Athletic trainers at high schools work to prevent and treat injuries that occur when students are practicing or competing in sporting events. Some trainers may also teach at the school as well.

- **Colleges and universities.** Athletic trainers for colleges and universities work with the athletic department to help maintain the health of college-level athletes, who train rigorously for highly competitive sports.

- **Professional sports.** An athletic trainer who works for a professional sports team will work within a particular sport, such as hockey, football, or baseball, and specialize in the injuries and training typical of that sport. While a team's season is only a few months long, athletic trainers work year round with professional athletes to help them maintain top physical performance and rehabilitate injuries in the off-season. This helps ensure that an athlete is prepared to return to play when the season begins. This particular work setting is very competitive due to the limited number of professional teams and the consequent small number of available athletic trainer jobs.

- **Sports medicine clinics.** Clinics are an opportunity for athletic trainers to gain experience working with different types of health care professionals. Clinics also

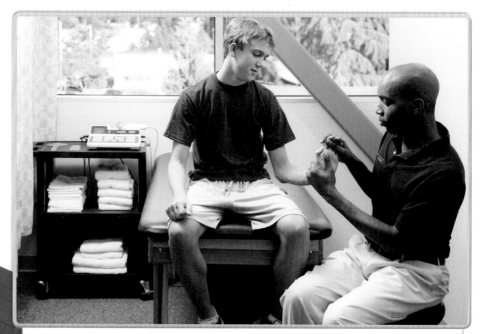

Athletic trainers work with athletes to determine the extent of an injury. They often oversee treatments, design rehabilitation plans, or recommend additional exercises to build strength.

provide services to secondary schools or teams who are unable to employ a full-time athletic trainer of their own. This setting allows athletic trainers to work with a diverse population of athletes from a variety of different sports.

- **Industrial settings.** Athletic trainers are now being employed by industrial companies to create injury prevention programs that help prepare workers for the physical demands of their jobs. Athletic trainers also provide injury assessment and rehabilitation services for workers who sustain an on-the-job injury.

- **Performing arts.** A lesser-known area in which athletic trainers are employed is the performing arts. Performing artists—dancers, actors, acrobats, circus performers, and others—often perform five to eight times a week. This frequency and intensity of performance can cause injury. Athletic trainers are relied upon to help keep performers in top physical condition.

CAREER ADVANCEMENT

Athletic trainers must keep themselves up-to-date on the latest medical advances, the most cutting-edge treatment techniques, and the newest developments in sports medi-

Tracking injuries and keeping accurate records of treatments and rehabilitation plans is a requirement for an athletic trainer.

cine. Not only does this help them with their current job, it also positions them for future advancement.

Earning an advanced degree, such as a doctorate in sports medicine or sports physiology, is also a great way to advance one's career. Many of the athletic trainers who work for professional sports team have doctorates. These advanced degrees require extensive research in a particular area of sports training, helping to establish these professionals as experts in their field.

Many athletic trainers begin their careers as assistants and work their way up to becoming a trainer. The

THE DIFFERENCE BETWEEN AN ATHLETIC TRAINER AND A PERSONAL TRAINER

Although the roles of athletic trainers and personal trainers sometimes overlap, these two professions are very different. While they share one common similarity—working with athletes—the requirements and job responsibilities vary greatly. Athletic trainers work alongside doctors to diagnose injuries. They then take responsibility for creating a rehabilitation program. In most states, athletic trainers must obtain a license to practice and hold a national certification from the National Athletic Trainers' Association. This certification requires professionals to meet specific educational and clinical requirements and to pass a comprehensive exam.

Personal trainers are fitness professionals who primarily work in health club settings. Unlike athletic trainers, they are not considered health care professionals. Personal trainers design workout programs to help individuals, including athletes, reach physical fitness goals. However, they are not qualified to diagnose or treat injuries. The field is much less rigorous and requires no formal education. Many personal trainers obtain certifications, but these are not required.

Below is an overview of the key differences between these two fields.

	ATHLETIC TRAINER	PERSONAL TRAINER
JOB DESCRIPTION	Expert at recognizing, treating, and preventing injury	Creates and monitors exercise programs to help individuals reach physical goals

	ATHLETIC TRAINER	PERSONAL TRAINER
EDUCATIONAL REQUIREMENTS	Educational requirements include at minimum a bachelor's degree and two years of clinical experience	No college-level education is required
CERTIFICATIONS	Must pass a comprehensive exam to become certified by the National Athletic Trainers' Association	May become certified by a number of organizations offering certifications in areas such as individual training or group training. Each organization sets varying education and practice requirements. Certification is not required for employment
MAJOR DUTIES	• Provide physical medicine and rehabilitation services • Prevent, diagnose, treat, and rehabilitate injuries • Coordinate care with physicians	• Assess fitness needs and design appropriate exercise regimens • Work with clients to achieve fitness goals • Work in health clubs and wellness centers where physical fitness activities take place

ultimate goal is often to become the head trainer with either a professional sports team or at a sports medicine clinic. Career advancement can take time, especially if one's desired outcome is to work for a professional sports team. These are among the most coveted positions, but also the most competitive. Because there are a limited number of professional sports teams, these jobs are very difficult to obtain. Very few athletic trainer positions become available each year.

For many athletic trainers, membership in the National Athletic Trainers' Association (NATA) is a must. This professional membership association is for certified athletic trainers and others who support the athletic training profession. The organization was founded in 1950 and has grown to include more than thirty thousand members worldwide. The majority of certified athletic trainers choose to be members of NATA, which provides professional support plus a wide selection of membership benefits. These include career advancement resources and professional development opportunities for trainers to help them further their knowledge and career options.

CAREER OUTLOOK

According to the Bureau of Labor Statistics' *Occupational Outlook Handbook*, the athletic training profession will see a 27 percent increase in employment through the year

2014. While the field may be growing, it is also changing to adapt to the newest technologies as medical equipment and techniques change and evolve. Athletic trainers will also see an increase in administrative duties and will work with a larger population of people as the profession expands in certain settings, such as high schools. As high school athletic programs continue to become more competitive and as the concern for the physical health of high school student-athletes grows, athletic trainers will likely see an increase in job opportunities and openings.

Chapter 5

PHYSICAL THERAPISTS

At the 2011 U.S. National Gymnastic Championships, defending national champion and six-time world medalist Rebecca Bross stepped up for her turn on the vault. When she landed, she dislocated her kneecap. Her coach immediately called for medical attention, and Bross was taken into the locker room for examination.

Bross would have surgery to reset and stabilize her kneecap, but her injury meant she would also spend several months in physical therapy, strengthening her knee before she could return to the gym. At her side during this entire process was a physical therapist. This health care professional designed a program to help Bross rehabilitate her knee so that she could return to training for the 2011 World Gymnasts competition and the 2012 London Olympics.

Rebecca Bross is carried off the event floor after falling on the vault during the first round of the U.S. national championships. Bross dislocated her kneecap and underwent physical therapy to strengthen her knee and leg before returning to training.

WHAT IS A PHYSICAL THERAPIST?

Physical therapists are health care professionals who help patients after they have sustained an injury. They help to restore function, improve mobility, relieve pain, and prevent or limit permanent physical disabilities. They can treat any part of the body that isn't functioning properly and are skilled in using stretching and strengthening techniques, balance and coordination exercises, and massage therapy to treat injuries and enhance mobility.

A physical therapist often begins treatment by testing and measuring a patient's strength, range of motion, balance and coordination, posture, muscle performance, respiration, and motor function. This gives the therapist a starting point to begin treatment and to establish the current condition of an injury. Once they examine their patients, physical therapists develop treatment plans to help improve the functionality of their injury. A treatment plan can include any number of methods and procedures, such as:

- Exercise, to improve a patient's flexibility, strength, endurance, range of motion, balance, and coordination

- Electrical stimulation, which uses an electrical current to force muscles to contract, helping to strengthen the muscles in and around the injured area

- Hot packs or cold compresses, both of which can help reduce pain and swelling and help muscles relax and stretch

- Ultrasound, which sends sound waves to generate heat within a body part. This loosens tissues and muscles to help them respond better to treatment and stimulate blood circulation

- Deep-tissue massage, which focuses on the deepest layers of muscles to relieve pain, increase blood circulation, and help with muscle movement

Physical therapists continuously document a patient's progress so that they can alter treatments if necessary or conclude treatment once an injury has fully healed.

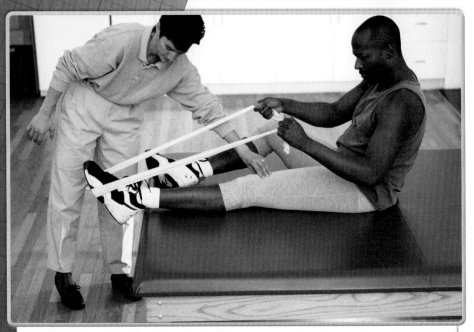

A physical therapist (PT) works with an athlete to increase flexibility and strength after an injury. PTs often use leg bands, weights, and exercise machines during rehabilitative treatments.

Physical therapists work with two different types of injuries: acute and chronic. Acute injuries occur suddenly and can usually be healed completely in less than six months. These types of injuries are common in sports and include broken bones, torn ligaments and tendons, sprains, and muscle strains. Chronic injuries are those that develop over time and take longer to treat and heal. For athletes, who put their bodies through the repeated stress of training and competing, these types of injuries can derail a career. Tendinitis and stress fractures are two of the most common injuries in sports and require longer periods of treatment before they heal.

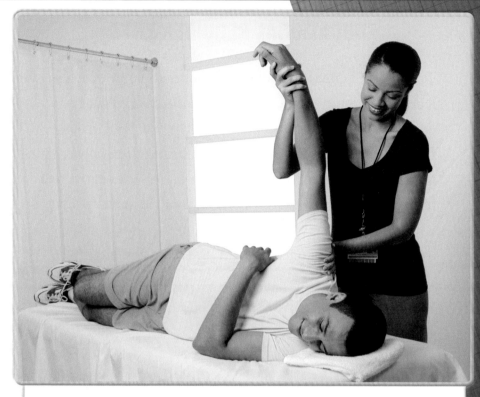

Stretching is an important part of physical therapy treatment. It helps strengthen muscles, relieve soreness, and increase range of motion.

Physical therapy is a physically demanding job. Therapists must constantly bend over, kneel, and squat while tending to their patients. They also spend hours at a time on their feet. Because they work with patients who have limited mobility, physical therapists do a lot of lifting. They help patients stand, hold them upright during certain treatments, and use their own bodies to help support the weight of their patients during therapeutic exercises.

EDUCATIONAL REQUIREMENTS

To work as a physical therapist, one needs to attend college and major in physical therapy. In the past, a bachelor's degree was sufficient to obtain work in the field. Today, however, nearly all physical therapy jobs require a master's or doctorate degree. Since 2000, the bachelor's degree in physical therapy has largely been eliminated and replaced with new programs that combine the bachelor and doctorate degrees into one program. Students complete both

A NEW CAREER FIELD: PHYSICAL THERAPY ASSISTANTS

A physical therapist assistant (PTA) provides therapeutic services under the direction and supervision of a licensed physical therapist. This new career field is just emerging as the educational standards for physical therapists change. Now, physical therapists are required to obtain an advanced degree. For those who aren't yet ready for graduate school, but want to work in the physical therapy field, becoming a physical therapy assistant is a great opportunity. Like physical therapists, PTAs help people of all ages who have injuries, medical problems, or other health conditions that impact their ability to move. Working in a sports medicine setting also allows PTAs to pick up exercise rehabilitation skills, allowing them to become experts in a particular area of physical therapy.

degrees in a six- or seven-year program before they can begin applying for work as a physical therapist. According to the American Physical Therapy Association (APTA), the majority of practicing physical therapists will have a doctorate degree by the year 2020.

Physical therapy programs include course work in biology, chemistry, physics, biomechanics, neuro-anatomy, abnormal psychology, kinesiology, human growth and development, human physical development, manifestations of disease, examination techniques, clinical procedures, and therapeutic procedures. After the completion of the course work portion of the program, a significant amount of a physical therapist's remaining education is gained through clinical rotations. These provide hands-on practice in treatment and exam techniques in settings such as hospitals and clinics. Clinical rotations include acute care, pediatrics, sports medicine, and outpatient orthopedics.

All physical therapists must pass a national licensing exam offered by the American Physical Therapy Association. Physical therapists are licensed in all fifty states and the District of Columbia. To meet the professional education requirement for licensure as a physical therapist, educational programs need to be accredited by the APTA. To be eligible to sit for the national exam, candidates must have at least a master's degree in the field.

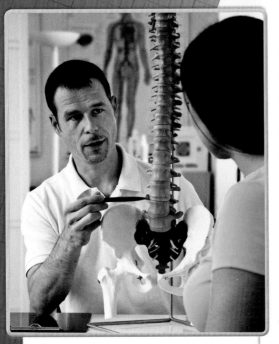

Understanding our own injuries can help us prevent additional damage to a problem area. Here, a physical therapist explains a back injury to a patient.

To gain experience in the field, getting a part-time job in a physical therapy clinic is a good starting point. The most likely position available will be that of a physical therapy aide. Aides work closely with and assist physical therapists and perform much of the same work. It's a great way to learn the ins and outs of the job.

The required clinical rotations are another way to gain experience in the various areas of physical therapy. Students work under the supervision of licensed professionals. Though these placements are unpaid, they are full of opportunities for students to talk to professionals about the field and gain valuable hands-on experience. The contacts you make during your rotations may very well lead to a job when you graduate.

If sports medicine is not an area offered by your college, an internship with a college sports team or a professional sports organization will provide good experience.

It also gives you a chance to explore the field and test your interest in it and aptitude for the work. Contacting schools or sports organizations directly or visiting the American Physical Therapy Association Web site will help you learn about available physical therapy internships.

Like most careers in health care, a physical therapist's education never stops. Some states require physical therapists to participate in continuing education to maintain licensure. Also, the national licensing exam must be taken every six years. In general, as cutting-edge technology, medical advances, and innovations in treatment techniques are continuously developed, physical therapists will need to participate in continuing education courses, workshops, and professional development opportunities throughout their career.

WHERE WILL I WORK?

Physical therapists who work in sports medicine find themselves interacting directly with professional, collegiate, high school, and recreational athletes. Hospitals, rehabilitation centers, college and professional sports teams, and high schools all employ physical therapists. Some of the most common places for physical therapists with a sports medicine specialization to work are:

- **Private practice outpatient clinics:** Many athletes visit a physical therapist a few times

Physical therapists work in clinics, private practice, hospitals, and nursing homes, and for professional sports teams. They work with patients young and old and with a variety of injuries.

a week for treatment. Outpatient clinics are often privately owned and may specialize in certain types of physical therapy, such as sports rehabilitation services.

- **Rehabilitation centers:** Oftentimes a sports team will contract with a rehabilitation center and use its physical therapists on a case-by-case basis. This type of care facility employs physical therapists as well as occupational, recreational, and speech therapists, so patients can get all the services they need in one place.

- **Secondary schools:** Many public and private schools hire physical therapists to work with their sports teams to help treat injuries that occur during practice or competition.

CAREER ADVANCEMENT

For a physical therapist, there are some opportunities to advance depending on where you are employed. If you work for a hospital or a large health care agency, you could move into a management or administrative position. This would require you to oversee other physical therapists and medical personnel. Two additional ways to advance your career are to go into private practice or to specialize in a particular areas of physical therapy, such as sports rehabilitation. Finally, teaching at the college level or doing

MOST COMMON SPORTS INJURIES TREATED BY PHYSICAL THERAPISTS

1. **LOWER BACK STRAIN:** Nearly all athletes experience some form of back strain from twisting awkwardly, lifting a heavy weight, or performing an unpracticed exercise. These injuries are due to weak or tense muscles, which can cause a pull or tear in the tendons in the back.

2. **TWISTED ANKLE:** Ankle twists or sprains happen when the foot turns inward and stretches or tears the ligaments on the outside of the ankle. This common injury occurs when running, jumping, or turning quickly.

3. **SHOULDER INJURY:** This type of injury is the most common for athletes competing in sports in which overhead movements are necessary. It's also an injury caused by overuse of the muscles, which can loosen the tendons that surround the shoulder, causing pain, stiffness, and weakness.

4. **NECK STRAIN:** This injury usually occurs on one side of the neck and causes pain when the head is turned from left to right. Neck strain can also occur from holding one's head in the same position for extended periods of time during an activity. Cyclists and mountain bikers commonly experience this injury.

5. **TENNIS ELBOW:** While not exclusively caused by playing tennis, tennis elbow refers to the inflammation of the tendons in the forearm. It is caused by repetitive movements.

6. **MUSCLE PULL:** A pull can occur in almost any muscle

from strain, overuse, fatigue, or falling.

7. **SHIN SPLINTS:** Brought on by jumping or running on hard surfaces, shin splints can cause pain in the muscles around the shin bones and can make it feel as though the shin bone itself is hurting.

8. **RUNNER'S KNEE:** This injury is caused from overuse that leads to irritation in the knee cap or its surrounding area.

A physical therapist helps a woman increase her balance using a balance board. Often, physical therapists will utilize sports equipment to help build strength and muscle conditioning.

academic and clinical research will help set you apart from other professionals in the field.

CAREER OUTLOOK

The fastest-growing specialty area in physical therapy is sports medicine. In general, the physical therapy field is expected to grow much faster than the average employment level in other fields. Employment is projected to grow by 30 percent from 2008 to 2018. In fact, *US News & World Report* named the field an excellent career choice as regards future prospects. The demand for physical therapists will continue to rise as more people become physically active in recreational sports. People over the age of fifty are becoming increasingly active. They are traveling, working out, and getting involved in sports. This will increase the need for physical therapists as these older athletes experience injuries that require treatment.

Chapter 6

SPORTS PSYCHOLOGISTS

After winning the Heisman Trophy, the most coveted award for a college football player, Ricky Williams's dream of playing professional football came true when the New Orleans Saints drafted him in 1999. When Williams, who always thought of himself as a shy person, began wearing his helmet during media interviews so reporters couldn't look closely at him, he realized that he had developed something more severe and serious than a normal case of shyness and nerves. The problem worsened when fans approached him for autographs. He would literally run in the opposite direction. Williams sought help from a sports psychologist. This health care professional diagnosed him with a social anxiety disorder and helped him manage the pressures of being an All-Star athlete.

WHAT IS A SPORTS PSYCHOLOGIST?

According to the American Psychological Association, sport psychology is the "scientific study of the

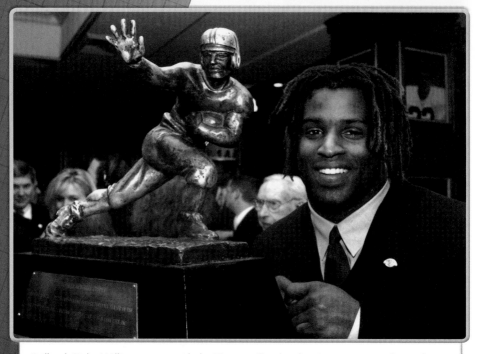

Tailback Ricky Williams poses with the Heisman Trophy, the most prestigious honor for a college football player. Williams turned to a sports psychologist when social anxiety issues began affecting his performance on and off the field.

psychological factors that are associated with participation and performance in sport, exercise, and other types of physical activity." A sports psychologist can help an athlete deal with the many emotional struggles he or she may face, whether the challenge is a mental disorder or the wide range of emotions that can occur when an athlete becomes injured. Injuries can make athletes feel angry, disappointed, frustrated, and sad. They may feel that the injury is unfair. They could be in denial or even experience depression. Their motivation can quickly evaporate if they need to halt their training program to take the time to rehabilitate an injury. Dealing with these mental and physical setbacks is what a sports psychologist does.

For Williams, meeting with a sport psychologist helped him work through the stresses that come from being a professional athlete. A sports psychologist works with athletes to help them deal with the demands of competition and training. They often counsel athletes on how to cope with the pressures of competing. They also assist with the psychological and emotional aspects of injuries, which can derail an athlete both physically and mentally. In addition, they advise coaches on how to boost athletes' motivation and team spirit.

Sports psychology is a rapidly growing profession, and many athletes seek the services of psychologists who can help them with the mental aspects of sports training. Research has found that these intensive levels of training require a certain mental toughness. Professional athletes, Olympians, and other elite competitors must develop and maintain their physical skills. Sports psychologists help athletes develop mental training skills to increase their focus, help them relax, and assist them in setting realistic goals. Mental toughness is as crucial an aspect of success in sports as physical toughness and ability.

Sports psychologists also study how exercise and participation in sports influences our psychological development, health, and well-being. Three major areas in the field are: applied sports psychology, clinical sports

Sports psychologist Gio Valiante's ground-breaking research became the new standard in golf psychology. Valiante not only works with golfers to improve their game, he also serves as the mental game consultant to the Golf Channel, *Golf Digest*, and the University of Florida.

psychology, and academic sports psychology.

Applied sports psychology focuses on teaching coping skills to enhance athletic performance, such as goal setting and visualization techniques. Visualization can help an athlete "see" himself or herself successfully executing a particular athletic task, such as catching a pass thrown by a quarterback or completing a challenging gymnastics routine. Clinical sports psychology combines mental training strategies from sports psychology with psychotherapy to help clients who suffer from mental health problems, including eating disorders and depression.

SPORTS SUPERSTITIONS AND RITUALS

Were the Boston Red Sox really cursed when Babe Ruth was traded to the New York Yankees in 1920? Does growing a beard enhance your odds of winning? Is there a jinx to appearing on the cover of *Sports Illustrated*?

Sports superstitions are as old as sport itself. But is there any truth to them? After all, the Boston Red Sox didn't win a World Series for eighty-six years, Bjorn Borg won five consecutive Wimbledon tennis championships when he grew a beard, and a large number of athletes have suffered curious misfortunes after appearing on the cover of the famed sports magazine.

A sports superstition arises when fans or athletes try to establish simplistic cause and effect to a highly complex interaction of random occurrences and flawed human efforts. Fans think they recognize a pattern of behavior and athletes notice certain coincidences—like what they ate, wore, did, or said on the day of a win or loss—and suddenly these seemingly simply acts are attributed to success or failure. The resulting rituals that are developed can sometimes be confidence builders for athletes, and they can appear to determine the difference between winning and losing. How athletes use rituals is an exciting area of research in sports psychology. Knowing that confidence is a large component of athletic success, psychologists are studying the influence of superstition and ritual on performance.

In some sports, such as figure skating, gymnastics, and wrestling, the pressure to be thin and/or below a certain target weight can be overwhelming. Academic sports psychologists can help athletes balance these pressures. Academic sports psychologists teach at colleges and universities and conduct research that helps guide treatments used by therapists who actively counsel athletes.

What exactly do sports psychologists do on a daily basis? In general, they mentally train athletes. This can include meeting regularly with the athlete to discuss problems or challenges he or she is facing, diagnosing psychological conditions such as performance anxiety and social disorders, treating conditions, helping the athlete cope with stress or loss of focus, and understanding and talking through the athlete's particular emotional problems.

EDUCATIONAL REQUIREMENTS

Sports psychologists need to earn a bachelor's degree in psychology and complete a graduate degree in counseling, clinical psychology, or therapy. In order to become a licensed clinical or counseling psychologist, a doctorate degree is required. There are two different types of doctorate degrees, a Ph.D. and a Psy.D.

A Ph.D. (doctor of philosophy) is a research-based degree that qualifies graduates to work in the field of clinical or counseling psychology. Earning a Ph.D. also allows

Many sports psychologists teach at the university level and work in clinics where they can coordinate their efforts with medical professionals in other disciplines.

psychologists to teach at the university level and conduct research. They can also practice at mental health clinics, hospitals, schools, private industries, government offices, and private practices. A Psy.D. (doctor of psychology) is a practice-based degree than enables a psychologist to work in both hospital and clinic settings and in private practice.

While there are very few graduate-level sports psychology programs (it is not one of the traditional fields of practice offered by graduate programs), the field is growing. For those who do not major directly in sports psychology, experience can be gained by combining a graduate level psychology degree with internships with sports organizations.

The American Board of Sport Psychology offers several professional certifications for sports psychologists. The highest-level credential is the board certified sports psychologist-diplomat, which "…signifies that the holder has advanced training and experience in sport psychology and is especially aware of ethical, methodological, and research issues associated with the application of methods to enhance the psychological performance of athletes."

Some sports psychologists are also accredited by one of a number of professional organizations. The Association for the Advancement of Applied Sport Psychology offers a certification called the designation as a certified consultant. A benefit of this certification is being listed on the U.S. Olympic Committee Sport Psychology Registry. This is a listing of sports psychologists approved to work with Olympic athletes and national teams.

WHERE WILL I WORK?

Sport psychologists work in a variety of settings and with a diverse range of clients. Most sport psychologists combine therapy practices with teaching and research. Some hold full-time positions with professional sports teams or national governing bodies (such as the U.S. Olympic Committee), while others work as full-time sport psychologists in private

Sports psychologists are often found working with elite athletes on the sidelines. They help athletes cope with the stress of intensive physical training and arm them with the mental training skills needed for focus, motivation, and mental toughness.

practice who see athletes referred to them by coaches and athletic trainers.

Sports psychologists work with elite competitors (at the professional, college, Olympic, and even high school levels). They may be employed by professional sports teams, college athletic departments, or, more rarely, by high schools. Many enter into private practice and consult with teams on a case-by-case basis.

The typical working environment for sports psychologists varies depending on the type of employer. Working for a professional sports team can be a demanding

THE RULES OF SPORTS PSYCHOLOGY

1. **PROCESS OVER OUTCOME:** Maintaining a consistent focus on the performance aspects of their sport will help athletes reach a positive outcome. Instead of placing an emphasis on the end result, focusing on necessary skills while playing will help athletes reach their goal.

2. **DEVELOP PRECOMPETITION ROUTINES:** Well-crafted routines help place athletes in the right mind-set before competition. They help give athletes confidence that their preparation is complete and they are ready to play.

3. **ASSOCIATE WITH GOOD PEOPLE AND METHODS:** To excel in sports, one must work hard for many years. Surrounding oneself with the right people will help develop the necessary skills needed to succeed in a sport.

4. **USE VISUALIZATION STRATEGIES:** Many elite athletes can make quick decisions while competing. This isn't luck. It's preparation. These athletes have thought through different scenarios and have decided that if a certain event happens, they will respond in a particular way. Athletes can "see" themselves training and competing successfully. Imagery can help athletes learn new skills, practice old ones, and achieve success. If you can "see" yourself winning a gold medal, you are giving yourself the confidence to do it.

5. **WHETHER YOU THINK YOU CAN OR CAN'T, YOU WILL:** In other words, if you think you're going to fail, you will. Positive thinking can be the difference between winning and losing.

6. **SET GOALS:** By establishing what they want to accomplish—running a faster 100 meter time, hitting the

most home runs, or scoring the most points—athletes can motivate themselves and focus their efforts during competition.

7. YOU MAKE YOUR OWN CHOICES: You can choose to commit to a goal, or let it go. By making a choice, you decide how you are going to perform.

8. PRACTICE MAKES PERFECT: It might be an age-old saying, but it's true. The more you practice the better your skills become—whether the skills are performance related or mental.

9. HAVE FUN: It might sound silly, but looking forward to challenging situations, working hard, and enjoying yourself can help you relax and perform better.

environment. A team sports psychologist may treat a large number of athletes and may be required to travel to games and competitions. Other environments, such as private practice, allow a psychologist to maintain his or her own daily schedule of appointments.

CAREER ADVANCEMENT

As sports psychologists advance in their career, they gain experience in a variety of areas by treating many different conditions. Psychologists can advance their careers by

Dr. Patrick Cohn is a world-renowned golf psychology expert who specializes in treating the mental barriers that can appear as a result of the demands of competing on the professional golf circuit.

completing research studies and identifying new treatment techniques, or they may develop an expertise in a particular area of sports psychology. For example, Dr. Patrick Cohn is a golf psychology expert and specializes in treating the mental barriers that occur as a result of the demands of competing on the professional golf circuit. Those psychologists in private practice may treat a wide variety of sports clients from any number of sports, or they may decide to specialize in particular kinds of injuries or particular sports.

CAREER OUTLOOK

The sports psychology field is growing. This means that more jobs will become available as professional sports teams, colleges, and even high schools recognize the benefits of having a sports psychologists on their athletic staffs.

Chapter 7
STRENGTH AND CONDITIONING COACHES

Heather Mason is the head strength and conditioning coach for the women's athletics department at the University of Tennessee. She is responsible for training all eleven of the school's women's athletic teams. Under her guidance, the university's strength and conditioning program has emerged as one of the best in the nation. Mason developed a training system that incorporates resistance training with conditioning exercises that include plyometrics, speed work, and aerobic/anaerobic training. Her program emphasizes two goals: maximizing strength and power to increase sports performance and decreasing the likelihood and severity of injury.

Mason earned a bachelor's degree in biology and a master's degree in sports administration. She is certified by the National Collegiate Strength and Conditioning Coaches Association. Her work at the University of Tennessee earned her the prestigious Master Strength & Conditioning Coach certification.

WHAT IS A STRENGTH AND CONDITIONING COACH?

So what exactly do strength and conditioning coaches like Heather Mason do? Under the direction of an organization's athletic trainer or athletic director, strength and conditioning coaches implement, conduct, and monitor athletes' strength and conditioning. They assist with the rehabilitation of injured athletes and often manage strength and conditioning facilities. They design strength programs that utilize different types of exercises to increase athletic performance and decrease the potential for injury. They also incorporate exercises that enhance athletes' skills, as well as their balance, coordination, quickness, and physical fitness—all of which contribute to an athlete's overall performance.

Strength and conditioning coaches plan, organize, and conduct practice sessions. They provide training direction, encouragement, and motivation in order to prepare athletes for competitive events. They create training programs for teams as a whole and tailor those programs by sport. For example, a soccer team may need more endurance conditioning than a basketball team, which might need a stronger focus on quickness. Strength and conditioning coaches also create plans for individual athletes who may need to strengthen a particular set of skills.

A strength and conditioning coach designs training drills to help athletes increase their agility, strength, and speed, and, ultimately, prevent injury.

Often these coaches will also arrange and conduct training camps, skill-improvement courses, clinics, and preseason workouts and tryouts. Many times strength and conditioning coaches are responsible for the athletic facilities in which their athletes train. As a result, they select fitness and training equipment and monitor athletes' use of equipment to ensure it is being utilized properly and safely.

An exciting aspect of being a strength and conditioning coach is observing the concrete results of his or her efforts. A strength and conditioning coach can witness athletes' performances improve thanks to his or her program, whether it's a lower time on the track for a runner, better endurance for a football player, improved coordination for a hockey player, or better balance for a gymnast.

EDUCATIONAL REQUIREMENTS

Strength and conditioning coaches have a variety of educational backgrounds. Commonly many choose to obtain a bachelor's degree in exercise science, health science, kinesiology, physical education, or physiology. These pro-

Targeted exercises can help prepare athletes for particular movements they may routinely perform as part of their sport. Strong and flexible knees, for example, help cut down on injuries in basketball when players pivot quickly to change directions.

grams all provide students with the course work they need. Students must gain knowledge in anatomy and physiology, exercise physiology, kinesiology and biomechanics, nutrition, scientific principals of strength and conditioning, resistance training and conditioning, exercise technique and exercise prescription, and program design for strength and conditioning. Many professionals also earn master's degrees to explore a particular area of the field in more depth or to help advance their careers. Advanced degrees in strength and conditioning, exercise physiology, exercise science, or sports administration are all popular choices.

Becoming certified as a strength and conditioning coach is a necessity. There are two main organizations that offer certifications for strength and conditioning coaches: the National Strength and Conditioning Association (NSCA) and the National Academy of Sports Medicine (NASM). Each of these organizations has different specialties.

The National Strength and Conditioning Association is an authority on strength and conditioning and its application to improving athletic performance and fitness. The association offers two certifications, the certified strength and conditioning specialist and the certified personal trainer. These certifications ensure that professionals in the field are knowledgeable in areas such as exercise science, testing and evaluation, exercise tech-

TEN QUALITIES OF A SUCCESSFUL STRENGTH AND CONDITIONING COACH

Rob Oviatt is the strength and conditioning coach for the University of Montana's football program. He is a thirty-year veteran of the field and a member of the Collegiate Strength and Conditioning Coaches Association, where he served as the organization's president from 2004 to 2008. He was also selected to the USA Strength & Conditioning Coach Hall of Fame in June of 2002. Oviatt is an ambassador for the field of strength and conditioning and has put together his own top ten qualities typical of a successful strength and conditioning coach:

1. Have a vision; then plan for everything.

2. Be a student of people. It's a people business.

3. Be consistent, honest, and punctual when dealing with everyone and every situation.

4. Sell your philosophy to your sport coaches and athletes.

5. Your loyalty and integrity are paramount.

6. There is always a way; you just have to find it.

7. The athletes must know you sincerely care about them.

8. Be yourself. Coach within your personality.

9. Continually educate yourself. Nobody knows it all.

10. You must respect and love the profession.

nique, program design, program organization, and fitness administration. The CSCS certification identifies individuals as possessing the necessary knowledge, skills, techniques, and expertise to be effective strength and conditioning coaches at the collegiate and/or professional level.

The National Academy of Sports Medicine is a leader in providing certifications and advanced credentials to health and fitness professionals. The organization offers four certifications: the performance enhancement specialist, the certified personal trainer, the corrective exercise specialist, and the stretch specialist. These certificates provide advanced qualifications to strength and conditioning professionals.

For more experienced professionals who already have spent several years working in the field, an advanced certification is offered. The Master Strength & Conditioning Coach certification is the highest honor one can achieve in the field. It represents one's commitment, professionalism, knowledge, experience, expertise, and longevity as a strength and conditioning professional.

WHERE WILL I WORK?

Strength and conditioning coaches work with a wide range of athletes, from elite professional and Olympic athletes to high school and college competitors. Professional

Some conditioning coaches volunteer their time to schools that cannot afford to hire them full-time. Many high schools utilize volunteers as part of their coaching staff.

sports organizations, colleges and universities, and high schools all employ strength and conditioning coaches. Some coaches even open private practices and contract their services to teams that cannot afford to have a full-time professional on staff.

The biggest opportunities for strength and conditioning coaches are in college sports, due simply to the sheer number of colleges and universities that have large athletic departments. The National Collegiate Athletic Association oversees twenty-three college-level sports, and thousands of schools are members of the NCAA. While there are only so many professional athletic teams, there are an abundance of colleges that offer athletic programs and need strength and conditioning coaches to aid in the training of their athletes.

The second largest source of employment opportunities is with professional sports teams. In particular, Major League Baseball (MLB) teams seem to offer the largest number of strength and conditioning jobs, though many open positions are internships with minor league teams. In baseball, one generally goes from being an intern with a minor league team, to a minor league coordinator, to a major league team head strength and conditioning coach.

In other professional sports, such as the National Basketball Association (NBA), the National Football League (NFL), Major League Soccer (MLS), and the National Hockey League (NHL), there are few if any minor league positions available. The most common path to promotion is to become an intern with a professional team and eventually advance to an assistant. Once an assistant, the next step is to become a coordinator. Coordinators often have interns or assistants working under them. Coordinator positions give professionals a chance to not only train athletes, but also to help manage other staff. This is an important experience to gain if one is to become a head strength and conditioning coach. This path of career advancement is similar to that pursued by college-level strength and conditioning coaches.

Joe Juraszek, a strength and conditioning coach for the Dallas Cowboys football team, works with a player as he tosses ropes during a strength drill.

NFL teams typically have one head strength and conditioning coach and one or two assistants. A recent trend sees many professional teams hiring a speed coach instead of an assistant strength and conditioning coach. A speed coach is a strength and conditioning coach who is also an expert in the training and techniques used to increase an athlete's speed. Because of the 16 game regular season schedule (as opposed to the 80 or more games played by each NBA and NHL team and the over 160 games played by MLB teams), NFL jobs require the least amount of travel. NFL strength and conditioning coaches also often have the most authority over the actual training the athletes engage in.

There are far fewer job opportunities at the high school level, and the availability of positions varies by state and even by school. In some states, such as Texas, California, and Ohio, strength and conditioning coaching jobs are fairly common in high schools. But in general, high school–level positions are often filled by volunteers, assistant coaches, or subcontracted employees who fill part-time positions. Often these are unpaid jobs.

CAREER ADVANCEMENT

Strength and conditioning coaches often begin their careers by volunteering or interning with a college sports team in either the weight room or as an assistant to the strength coaches. While pursing a graduate degree, many students find work as a graduate assistant with a sports team. In this position, one can learn the daily routine of a strength and conditioning coach and make professional contacts in the field. It's common for an intern or graduate assistant to be hired by the sports team he or she interned or volunteered with. Once in the door, advancement becomes easier, with professionals often being promoted from within an organization.

Advancing in the field often means going into sports administration. Here one will manage other sports professionals or design an overall program implemented by others, as is the case with Heather Mason at the University of Tennessee. By earning her master's degree in sports administration, she worked her way up to becoming the assistant athletics director and the director of strength and conditioning at the school.

CAREER OUTLOOK

According to the Bureau of Labor Statistics, job prospects over the next decade are expected to be good for strength and conditioning coaches. Opportunities are strong because demand for experienced and knowledgeable trainers is expected to remain high in health clubs, fitness facilities, and other settings in which fitness workers are concentrated. Competition is high for high-profile and in-demand professional- and college-level positions. Through natural attrition (mainly retirement), however, jobs will still become available at this level.

COLLEGE AND UNIVERSITY PROGRAMS IN SPORTS FITNESS AND MEDICINE

The following is a list of a number of colleges and universities that offer programs in sports fitness and medicine:

Baylor University
Waco, Texas
Programs of study: athletic training, business (sports, sponsorship and sales), exercise physiology, recreation, physical education, nutrition sciences, psychology, pre-physical therapy, pre-physician assistant, pre-medicine

Boston University
Boston, Massachusetts
Programs of study: Athletic training, athletic training/physical therapy, human physiology, nutritional sciences, physical therapy, psychology

Central Michigan University
Mount Pleasant, Michigan
Programs of study: athletic training/sports medicine, exercise science, sports studies

Marietta College
Marietta, Ohio
Programs of study: health science, psychology, physician assistant

Missouri State University
Springfield, Missouri
Programs of study: athletic training, physical education, physical therapy, physician assistant studies, sports medicine

Norwich University
Northfield, Vermont
Programs of study: athletic training, physical education, psychology, sports medicine/health sciences

The Ohio State University
Columbus, Ohio
Programs of study: Athletic training, sports industry, sports/commercial turf

equipment, pre-medicine, pre-physical therapy, psychology, nutrition

Quinnipiac University
Hamden, Connecticut
Programs of study: athletic training/sports medicine, physical therapy, physician assistant

Stanford University
Palo Alto, California
Programs of study: Sport medicine fellowship

University of Colorado, Denver
Denver, Colorado
Programs of study: pre-health studies (pre-physical therapy, pre-physician assistant), psychology, management and organization (sports and entertainment management), physician assistant, psychology

University of Miami
Coral Gables, Florida
Programs of study: athletic training, exercise physiology, physical therapy, psychology, sport administration

University of Michigan, Ann Arbor
Ann Arbor, Michigan
Programs of study: athletic training, movement science, physical education, psychology, sport management

University of North Dakota
Grand Forks, North Dakota
Programs of study: athletic training, athletic coaching, dietetics, nutrition, physical education/exercise science/wellness, physical therapy, physician assistant, psychology, rehabilitation and human services, sports business

University of Pittsburgh
Pittsburgh, Pennsylvania
Programs of study: physical therapy, rehabilitation science and technology, sports medicine and nutrition

University of South Florida
Tampa, Florida
Programs of study: athletics training/sports medicine, physical education, psychology

University of Tennessee at Chattanooga
Chattanooga, Tennessee
Programs of study: exercise science, nutrition/dietetics, food and nutrition, sports and leisure service administration, psychology, rehabilitation sciences

University of Virginia
Charlottesville, Virginia
Programs of study: sport and exercise psychology, sports medicine/athletic training, exercise physiol-ogy, kinesiology

Utah State University
Logan, Utah
Programs of study: nutrition/dietetics/food science, psychology

West Chester University of Pennsylvania
West Chester, Pennsylvania
Programs of study: athletic training, health and physical education, exercise specialist, nutrition and dietetics, psychology

SPORTS PHYSICIANS

Academics

- Bachelor's degree

- Medical school

- Internship

- Medical residency

- Fellowship (for certain specialties, including sports medicine)

Experience

- Volunteer opportunities with local emergency response teams or ambulance corps

Career Paths

- Physicians can go into hospital administration.

- Some physicians become specialists in certain fields.

- Teaching at the college level is also an option.

Duties and Responsibilities

- Diagnose illnesses

- Prescribe and administer treatment

- Perform surgery

- Prescribe medication when necessary

ATHLETIC TRAINERS

Academics

- Bachelor's degree

- Master's degree

- Certifications needed

Experience

- Internships at the high school, college, or professional level

- Volunteering opportunities helpful

Career Paths

- Most first jobs are as assistants. Assistants become trainers; trainers advance to head trainer.

Duties and Responsibilities

- Prevent, diagnose, assess, treat, and rehabilitate muscle and bone injuries and illnesses

- Evaluate and assess injuries and provide immediate care when needed

- Educate athletes on reducing risk for injuries by the proper use of equipment

- Recommend exercises to improve balance

and strength, as well as home exercises and therapy programs

PHYSICAL THERAPISTS

Academics

- Graduate degree required

Experience

- Clinical experience is necessary and obtained while in school

Career Paths

- Physical therapists can become managers or hospital administrators

Duties and Responsibilities

- Diagnose and treat individuals who have medical problems or other health-related conditions, illnesses, or injuries that limit their ability to move and perform functional activities

- Develop a plan using treatment techniques to promote the ability to move, reduce pain, restore function, and prevent disability

SPORTS PSYCHOLOGISTS

Academics

- Bachelor's degree

- Master's degree or doctorate necessary

- Fellowship in sports psychology helpful

Experience

- Shadowing a counselor

- Volunteering for community organizations

Career Paths

- Work for a college or professional sports team

- Enter private practice

Duties and Responsibilities

- Diagnose and treat mental illness and social disorders

- Research behavioral patterns

STRENGTH AND CONDITIONING COACHES

Academics

- Many choose to obtain a bachelor's degree in exercise science, health science, kinesiology, physical education, or physiology. Many professionals also earn master's degrees to explore a particular area of the field in more depth or to help advance their careers. Advanced degrees in strength and conditioning, exercise physiology, exercise science, or sports administration are all popular choices. Becoming certified as a strength and conditioning coach is a necessity.

Experience

- Volunteering for a high school or college team; internship with a college or professional team

Career Paths

- Strength and conditioning coaches often begin their careers by volunteering or interning with a college sports team in either the weight room or as an assistant to the strength coaches. While pursing a graduate degree, many students find work as a graduate assistant with a sports team.

- It's common for an intern or graduate assistant to be hired by the sports team he or she interned or volunteered with.

- Once in the door, advancement becomes easier, with professionals often being promoted from within an organization.

- Advancing in the field often means going into sports administration, where one will manage other sports professionals or design an overall program implemented by others.

Duties and Responsibilities

- Implement, conduct, and monitor athletes' strength and conditioning.

- Assist with the rehabilitation of injured athletes and often manage strength and conditioning facilities.

- Design strength programs that utilize different types of exercises to increase athletic performance and decrease the potential for injury.

- Incorporate exercises that enhance an athlete's skills, as well as balance, coordination, quickness, and physical fitness.

- Plan, organize, and conduct practice sessions and provide training direction, encouragement, and motivation in order to prepare athletes for competitive events.

- Create training programs for teams as a whole and tailor those programs by sport. Create plans for individual athletes who may need to strengthen a particular set of skills.

- Arrange and conduct training camps, skill-improvement courses, clinics, and pre-season workouts and tryouts.

- Many strength and conditioning coaches are also responsible for the athletic facilities in which their athletes train. As a result, they select fitness and training equipment and monitor athletes' use of equipment to ensure it is being utilized properly and safely.

SPORTS PHYSICIANS

SIGNIFICANT POINTS

- Many physicians and surgeons work long, irregular hours.

- Acceptance to medical school is highly competitive.

- Formal education and training requirements—typically four years of undergraduate school, four years of medical school, and three to eight years of internship and residency—are among the most demanding of any occupation, but earnings are among the highest.

NATURE OF THE WORK

Physicians and surgeons diagnose illnesses and prescribe and administer treatment for people suffering from injury or disease. Physicians examine patients; obtain medical histories; and order, perform, and interpret diagnostic tests. They counsel patients on diet, hygiene, and preventive health care.

TRAINING

The common path to practicing as a physician requires eight years of education beyond high school and three to eight additional years of internship and residency. All states, the District of Columbia, and U.S. territories license physicians.

OTHER QUALIFICATIONS

People who wish to become physicians must have a desire to serve patients, be self-motivated, and be able to survive the pressures and long hours of medical education and practice. Physicians also must have a good bedside manner, emotional stability, and the ability to make decisions in emergencies. Prospective physicians must be willing to study throughout their career to keep up with medical advances.

ADVANCEMENT

Some physicians and surgeons advance by gaining expertise in specialties and subspecialties and by developing a reputation for excellence among their peers and patients. Physicians and surgeons may also start their own practice or join a group practice. Others teach residents and other new doctors, and some advance to supervisory and managerial roles in hospitals, clinics, and other settings.

JOB OUTLOOK

Employment of physicians and surgeons is projected to grow 22 percent from 2008 to 2018, much faster than the average for all occupations. Job growth will occur because of continued expansion of health care–related industries.

WORK ENVIRONMENT

Many physicians work in small private offices or clinics, often assisted by a small staff of nurses and other administrative personnel.

ATHLETIC TRAINERS

SIGNIFICANT POINTS

- A bachelor's degree is usually the minimum requirement, but many athletic trainers hold a master's or doctoral degree.

- Long hours, sometimes including nights and weekends, are common.

- Job prospects should be good in the health care industry and in high schools, but competition is expected for positions with professional and college sports teams.

NATURE OF THE WORK

Athletic trainers help prevent and treat injuries for people of all ages. Their patients and clients include everyone from professional athletes to industrial workers. Recognized by the American Medical Association as allied health professionals, athletic trainers specialize in the prevention, diagnosis, assessment, treatment, and rehabilitation of muscle and bone injuries and illnesses. Athletic trainers, as some of the first health care providers on the scene when injuries occur, must be able to recognize, evaluate, and assess injuries and provide immediate care when needed.

TRAINING

A bachelor's degree from an accredited college or university is required for almost all jobs as an athletic trainer.

OTHER QUALIFICATIONS

Athletic trainers deal directly with a variety of people, so they need good social and communication skills. They should be able to manage difficult situations and the stress associated with them, such as when disagreements arise with coaches, patients, clients, or parents regarding suggested treatment. Athletic trainers also should be organized, be able to manage time wisely, be inquisitive, and have a strong desire to help people.

ADVANCEMENT

Some athletic trainers advance by switching teams or sports to gain additional responsibility or pay. Assistant athletic trainers may become head athletic trainers and, eventually, athletic directors, physicians, or hospital or clinic practice administrators where they assume a management role. Some athletic trainers move into sales and marketing positions, using their expertise to sell medical and athletic equipment.

JOB OUTLOOK

Athletic trainers hold about 16,300 jobs and are found in every part of the country. Most athletic trainer jobs are related to sports, although an increasing number are also found in non-sports settings.

WORK ENVIRONMENT

The industry and individual employer are significant in determining the work environment of athletic trainers. Many athletic trainers work indoors most of the time; others, especially those in some sports-related jobs, spend much of their time working outdoors. The job also might require standing for long periods, working with medical equipment or machinery, and being able to walk, run, kneel, stoop, or crawl. Travel may be required.

PHYSICAL THERAPISTS

SIGNIFICANT POINTS

- Employment is expected to grow much faster than average.

- Job opportunities should be good.

- Today's entrants to this profession need a post-baccalaureate degree from an accredited physical therapist program.

- About 60 percent of physical therapists work in hospitals or in offices of other health practitioners.

NATURE OF THE WORK

Physical therapists are health care professionals who diagnose and treat individuals of all ages, from newborns to the very oldest, who have medical problems or other health-related conditions, illnesses, or injuries that limit their abilities to move and perform functional activities as well as they would like in their daily lives.

TRAINING

Today's entrants to this profession need a bachelor's degree from an accredited physical therapy program. All states regulate the practice of physical therapy, which usually requires passing scores on national and state examinations.

OTHER QUALIFICATIONS

Physical therapists should have strong interpersonal and communication skills so that they can educate patients about their condition and physical therapy treatments and communicate with patients' families. Physical therapists also should be compassionate and possess a desire to help patients.

ADVANCEMENT

Physical therapists are expected to continue their professional development by participating in continuing education courses and workshops. Some physical therapists become board certified in a clinical specialty. Opportunities for physical therapists exist in academia and research. Some become self-employed, providing contract services or opening a private practice.

JOB OUTLOOK

Employment of physical therapists is expected to grow by 30 percent from 2008 to 2018, much faster than the average for all occupations.

WORK ENVIRONMENT

Physical therapists practice in hospitals, outpatient clinics, and private offices that have specially equipped facilities. These jobs can be physically demanding because therapists may have to stoop, kneel, crouch, lift, and stand for long periods. In addition, physical therapists move heavy equipment and lift patients or help them turn, stand, or walk.

SPORTS PSYCHOLOGISTS

SIGNIFICANT POINTS

- About 34 percent of psychologists are self-employed, mainly as private practitioners and independent consultants.

- Employment growth will vary by specialty; for example, clinical, counseling, and school psychologists will have 11 percent growth; industrial-organizational psychologists, 26 percent growth; and 14 percent growth is expected for all other psychologists.

- Acceptance to graduate psychology programs is highly competitive.

- Job opportunities should be the best for those with a doctoral degree in a subfield, such as health; those with a master's degree will have good prospects in industrial-organization; bachelor's degree holders will have limited prospects.

NATURE OF THE WORK

Psychologists study mental processes and human behavior by observing, interpreting, and recording how people and other animals relate to one another and the environment. To do this, psychologists often look for patterns that will help them understand and predict behavior using scientific methods, principles, or procedures to test their ideas.

TRAINING

A master's or doctoral degree, and a license, are required for most psychologists.

OTHER QUALIFICATIONS

A specialist degree or its equivalent is required for certain specialties, such as sports psychology. Aspiring psychologists who are interested in direct patient care must be emotionally stable, mature, and able to deal effectively with people. Sensitivity, compassion, good communication skills, and the ability to lead and inspire others are particularly important qualities for people wishing to do clinical work and counseling.

ADVANCEMENT

Psychologists can improve their advancement opportunities by earning an advanced degree and by participation in continuing education. Many psychologists opt to start their own private practice after gaining experience working in the field.

JOB OUTLOOK

Employment of psychologists is expected to grow 12 percent from 2008 to 2018, about as fast as the average for all occupations.

WORK ENVIRONMENT

Psychologists' work environments vary by subfield and place of employment. For example, clinical, school, and counseling psychologists in private practice frequently have their own offices and set their own hours. However, they usually offer evening and weekend hours to accommodate their clients.

STRENGTH AND CONDITIONING COACHES

SIGNIFICANT POINTS

- These jobs require immense overall knowledge of both the game and the fitness routines and injuries most closely associated with it.

- Certification is required.

- Employment is expected to grow much faster than the average.

- Job prospects are expected to be good.

NATURE OF THE WORK

Strength and conditioning coaches lead, instruct, and motivate individuals or groups in exercise activities, including cardiovascular exercise, strength training, and stretching. They help athletes and clients assess their level of physical fitness and set and reach fitness goals. They also demonstrate various exercises and help clients improve their exercise techniques. They may keep records of their athletes' or clients' exercise sessions to monitor progress toward physical fitness. They also may advise their athletes or clients on how to modify their lifestyles to improve their general fitness.

TRAINING

Certification is required. Most certifying organizations require candidates to have a high school diploma, be certified in cardiopulmonary resuscitation (CPR), and pass an exam. All certification exams have a written component, and some also have a practical component. The exams measure knowledge of human physiology, understanding of proper exercise techniques, assessment of client fitness levels, and development of appropriate exercise programs. There is no particular training program required for certification; candidates may prepare however they prefer. Certifying organizations do offer study materials, including books, CD-ROMs, other audio and visual materials, and exam preparation workshops and seminars, but candidates are not required to purchase materials to take exams. A bachelor's degree in a field related to health or fitness, such as exercise science or physical education, is also recommended.

ADVANCEMENT

Strength and conditioning coaches often begin their careers by volunteering or interning with a college sports team in either the weight room or as an assistant to the strength coaches. While pursing a graduate degree, many students find work as a graduate assistant with a sports team. It's common for an intern or graduate assistant to be hired by the sports team he or she interned or volunteered with. Once in the door, advancement becomes easier, with professionals often being promoted from within an organization. Advancing in the field often means going into sports administration, where one will manage other sports professionals or design an overall program implemented by others.

JOB OUTLOOK

Employment of athletes, coaches, fitness specialists, and related workers is expected to grow much faster than the average for all occupations through 2018. Very keen competition is expected for jobs at the highest levels of sports with progressively more favorable opportunities in lower levels of competition.

WORK ENVIRONMENT

Irregular work hours are common for strength and conditioning coaches. They often work Saturdays, Sundays, evenings, and holidays. Full-time coaches usually work more than forty hours a week for several months during the sports season, if not most of the year. High school coaches in educational institutions often coach more than one sport. Strength and training coaches who participate in competitions that are held outdoors may be exposed to all weather conditions of the season. Most work days, however, are spent indoors in gyms and training facilities. Strength and conditioning coaches must frequently travel to sporting events.

GLOSSARY

acute In terms of fitness and medicine, the rapid onset of injury or illness.

aerobic Prolonged exercise of moderate intensity such as running or walking.

anaerobic Intense exercise used by athletes to promote strength, speed, and power. Weight training is an anaerobic exercise.

biology An area of science that studies life and living organisms.

biomechanics The study of the structure and function of biological systems by means of the methods of mechanics.

biotechnology A area of biology that involves the use of living organisms and bioprocesses in engineering, technology, and medicine.

cardiovascular Anything related to the heart and blood vessels.

chemistry A science that deals with the composition, structure, and properties of substances and with the transformations that they undergo.

chronic Marked by long duration or frequent recurrence.

doctorate The title, rank, or degree of doctor.

epidemic Widespread growth of a disease.

fellowship A position that offers extensive learning or experience in a particular area.

genetics A branch of biology that deals with the heredity and variation of organisms.

internal medicine A branch of medicine that deals with the diagnosis and treatment of diseases not requiring surgery.

internship Supervised practical career experience.

kinesiology The study of the principles of mechanics and anatomy in relation to human movement.

musculoskeletal The study of muscles and the skeletal structure.

neuroanatomy The study of nervous tissue and the nervous system.

obesity A condition characterized by the excessive accumulation and storage of fat in the body.

orthopedics A branch of medicine concerned with the correction or prevention of deformities, disorders, or injuries of the skeleton and associated structures, such as tendons and ligaments.

outpatient A patient who is not hospitalized overnight, but who visits a hospital, clinic, or associated facility for diagnosis or treatment.

pediatrics A branch of medicine dealing with the development, care, and diseases of children.

performing arts A branch of the arts in which artists uses their own body, face, and presence as a medium of expression.

physics A science that deals with matter and energy and their interactions.

physiology A branch of biology that deals with the functions and activities of life or of living matter (as organs, tissues, or cells) and of the physical and chemical phenomena involved.

Pilates An exercise regimen, created by Joseph H. Pilates, that uses special apparatuses and/or a person's own body weight to build strength and achieve fitness.

posture The upright position of the body.

professional development Educational opportunities offered to continue one's learning.

psychologist A person who studies the mind and human behavior.

psychology The science of mind and human behavior.

specialization A particular area of study.

stress fracture A hairline fracture, or cracking, of a bone caused by repeated use.

radiology A branch of medicine concerned with the use of radiant energy (e.g. X-rays) or radioactive material in the diagnosis and treatment of disease.

rehabilitation To restore to a former capacity; the process of returning to health.

respiratory Anything associated with breathing and the body system that controls breathing.

ultrasound Vibrations of sound used to create a two-dimensional image for the detection, diagnosis, and treatment of disease and injury.

FOR MORE INFORMATION

American Academy of Orthopaedic Surgeons (AAOS)
6300 North River Road
Rosemont, IL 60018
(847) 823-7186
Web site: http://www.aaos.org
The AAOS is the preeminent provider of musculoskeletal education to orthopaedic surgeons.

American College of Sports Medicine (ACSM)
401 West Michigan Street
Indianapolis, IN 46202-3233
(317) 637-9200
Web site: http://www.acsm.org
As the largest sports medicine and exercise science
organization in the world, ACSM has more than
twenty-thousand members worldwide.

American Medical Society for Sports Medicine (AMSSM)
4000 West 114th Street, Suite 100
Leawood, KS 66211
(913) 327-1415

Web site: http://www.amssm.org

The purpose of the American Medical Society for Sports Medicine is to foster a relationship among dedicated, competent sports medicine specialists and to provide a quality educational resource for AMSSM members, other sports medicine professionals, and the general public.

American Orthopaedic Society for Sports Medicine (AOSSM)

6300 North River Road, #500

Rosemont, IL 60018

(847) 292-4900

Web site: http://www.sportsmed.org

The American Orthopaedic Society for Sports Medicine is a world leader in sports medicine education, research, communication, and fellowship. AOSSM is an international organization of orthopaedic surgeons and other health professionals dedicated to sports medicine.

American Osteopathic Academy of Sports Medicine (AOASM)

7600 Terrace Avenue, Suite 203

Middleton, WI 53562

(608) 831-4400

Web site: http://www.aoasm.org

AOASM provides an educational resource for members,

health and sports medicine professionals, and the general public.

American Physical Therapy Association (APTA)
1111 North Fairfax Street
Alexandria, VA 22314-1488
(703) 684-2782
Web site: http://www.apta.org

The APTA is a membership-based organization that provides physical therapists with professional and educational resources and career information. The organization also acts as an advocacy group for its members and for the field of physical therapy as a whole.

Association for Applied Sport Psychology (AASP)
2424 American Lane
Madison, WI 53704
(608) 443-2475
Web site: http://www.appliedsportpsych.org

The AASP promotes the science and practice of sport and exercise psychology, advocates for psychological principles that have been supported by research, and is a leader in promoting and enhancing professional standards in the field of sport and exercise psychology.

Canadian Academy of Sport Medicine

180 Elgin Street, Suite 1400

Ottawa, ON K2P 2K3

Canada

(613) 748-5851

Web site: http://www.casm-acms.org

The Canadian Academy of Sport Medicine is an organization providing medical care to elite athletes at international events and is a leading source of information and expertise in the art and science of sport medicine.

Canadian Sport Massage Therapists Association (CSMTA)

1030 Burnside Road West

Victoria, BC V8Z 1N3

(250) 590-9861

Web site: http://www.csmta.ca

The CSMTA provides leadership in the field of sport massage therapy and education through the establishment of professional standards and qualifications of its members as a certifying body in Canada.

National Association of Sports Nutrition (NASN)

7710 Balboa Avenue, Suite 311

San Diego, CA 92111

(858) 694-0317

Web site: http://www.nasnutrition.com/

> The NASN promotes the field of sports nutrition and provides licensing, certification, and continuing education opportunities for members.

National Athletic Trainers' Association
2952 Stemmons Freeway, #200
Dallas, TX 75247
(214) 637.6282
Web site: http://www.nata.org/athletic-training

> The National Athletic Trainers' Association is the professional membership association for certified athletic trainers and others who support the athletic training profession.

WEB SITES

Due to the changing nature of Internet links, Rosen Publishing has developed an online list of Web sites related to the subject of this book. This site is updated regularly. Please use this link to access this list.

http://www.rosenlinks.com/gcsi/fit

FOR FURTHER READING

American Kinesiology Association. *Careers in Sport, Fitness and Exercise*. Champaign, IL: Human Kinetics, 2011.

Bickerstaff, Linda. *Careers in Nutrition*. New York, NY: Rosen Publishing, 2008.

Bijlefeld, Marjolijn, and Sharon K. Zoumbaris. *Food and You: A Guide to Healthy Habits for Teens*. Westport, CT: Greenwood Publishing Group, 2008.

Clover, Jim. *Sports Medicine Essentials: Core Concepts in Athletic Training & Fitness Instruction*. Florence, KY: Delmar Cengage Learning, 2007.

Dunford, Marie. *Fundamentals of Sport and Exercise Nutrition*. Champaign, IL: Human Kinetics, 2010.

Etnier, Jennifer L., and Dominy Alderman. *Bring Your "Game": A Young Athlete's Guide to Mental Toughness*. Chapel Hill, NC: The University of North Carolina Press, 2009.

Field, Shelly. *Career Opportunities in the Sports Industry*. New York, NY: Checkmark Books, 2010.

Floyd, Patricia A., and Beverly Allen. *Careers in Health, Physical Education, and Sports*. Pacific Cove, CA: Brooks Cole Publishing, 2008.

Horn, Geoffrey M. *Sports Therapist* (Cool Careers). New York, NY: Gareth Stevens Publishing, 2008.

Howell, Brian. *Sports* (Inside the Industry). Edina, MN: Essential Library, 2011.

KMS Publishing, Inc. *Establishing a Career in Sports Medicine: Plan Your Career in Sports Medicine Now and Enjoy the Many Possibilities For Personal Advancement It*

Offers. Charleston, SC: CreateSpace, 2010.

Kummer, Patricia K. *Sports Medicine Doctor* (Cool Careers). Ann Arbor, MI: Cherry Lake Publishing, 2008.

Reeves, Diane Lindsey, Lindsey Clasen, and Nancy Bond. *Career Ideas for Kids Who Like Sports.* New York, NY: Checkmark Books, 2007.

Siedentop, Daryl. *Introduction to Physical Education, Fitness, and Sport.* New York, NY: McGraw-Hill Humanities/ Social Sciences/Languages, 2008.

Williams, Melvin H. *Nutrition for Health, Fitness, and Sport.* New York, NY: McGraw-Hill Science/Engineering/Math, 2009.

Wolf, Robert. *Become a Certified Personal Trainer: Surefire Strategies to Pass the Major Certification Exams, Build a Strong Client List, and Start Making Money.* New York, NY: McGraw-Hill, 2009.

Wong, Glenn M. *The Comprehensive Guide to Careers in Sports.* Burlington, MA: Jones & Bartlett Publishers, 2008.

BIBLIOGRAPHY

Bracker, Mark D. *The 5-Minute Sports Medicine Consult*, Second Edition. Philadelphia, PA: Lippincott Williams & Wilkins, 2011.

Brukner, Peter, and Karim Khan. *Brukner & Khan's Clinical Sports Medicine*. Sydney, Australia: McGraw-Hill, 2011.

Cataletto, Mary E., et al. *Sports Medicine Board Review, Second Edition*. New York, NY: McGraw-Hill, 2006.

Cohen, Steven M. "10 Hot Sports Medicine Trends." Suite101.com. January 17, 2009. Retrieved September 2011 (http://www.suite101.com/content/10-hot-sports-medicine-trends-a90577).

Davis, Nate. "Peyton Manning has another neck surgery." *USA Today*. September 8, 2011. Retrieved September 2011 (http://content.usatoday.com/communities/thehuddle/post/2011/09/espn-colts-qb-peyton-man-ning-has-more-neck-surgery/1?csp=hf&loc=interstitialskip).

Education Portal. "Athletic Trainer: Summary of How to Become an Athletic Trainer." Retrieved August 2011 (http://educationportal.com/articles/Athletic_Trainer_Summary_of_How_to_Become_an_Athletic_Trainer.html).

Education Portal. "Best Sports Medicine Schools in the United States." Retrieved August 2011 (http://education-portal.com/best_sports_medicine_schools.html).

Education Portal. "Sports Medicine Doctor: Educational Requirements." Retrieved September 2011 (http://education-portal.com/articles/Sports_Medicine_Doctor_Educational_Requirements.html).

Education Portal. "Top Athletic Training Colleges in the U.S." Retrieved August 2011 (http://education-portal. com/athletic_training_colleges.html).

France, Robert C. *Introduction to Sports Medicine and Athletic Training.* Second edition. Florence, KY: Delmar Cengage Learning, 2010.

Higgins, Matt. "Doctors on the Scene Acted Quickly to Treat Everett with Cold Therapy." *New York Times.* September 16, 2007. Retrieved 2011 (http://www. nytimes.com/2007/09/16/sports/football/16everett .html).

Higgins, Richard, et al., eds. *Essential Sports Medicine.* Malden, MA: Blackwell Publishing, 2006.

Hoch, Bryan. "Hughes to See Physician After Setback." MLB.com., April 26, 2011. Retrieved August 2011 (http://mlb.mlb.com/ news/article.jsp?ymd=20110425&content_ id=18238178&vkey=news_nyy&c_id=nyy).

Housh, Terry J., Dona J. Housh, and Glen O. Johnson. *Introduction to Exercise Science.* Scottsdale, AZ: Holcomb Hathaway, 2007.

Howard, Thomas M., and Janus D. Butcher. *The Little Black Book of Sports Medicine.* Second edition. Sudbury, MA: Jones and Bartlett Publishers, 2006.

Karageorghis, Costas, and Peter Terry. *Inside Sport Psychology.* Champaign, IL: Human Kinetics, 2010.

Kissel, Chris. "Sports Medicine Career Options." Suite101.com., May 31, 2010. Retrieved September 2011 (http://www.suite101.com/content/ sports-medicine-careers-options-a243142).

KMS Publishing.com. *Establishing a Career in Sports Medicine.* Charleston, SC: CreateSpace, 2010.

Lin, Joseph. "Top 10 Sports Superstitions." *Time.,* June 10, 2010. Retrieved September 2011 (http://www.time.com/time/specials/packages/

article/0,28804,1995519_1995521_1995517,00.html).

Longman, Jere. "Wambach Breaks Leg in Exhibition" *New York Times.*, July 17, 2008. Retrieved August 2011 (http://www.nytimes.com/2008/07/17/sports/ olympics/17abby.html).

Madden, Christopher, et al. *Netter's Sports Medicine* (Netter Clinical Science). Philadelphia, PA: Saunders, 2010.

Madden, Kaitlin. "What It's Like to Be an Athletic Trainer in the NFL: Q&A with Leigh Weiss." AOL.com., December 20, 2010. Retrieved August 2011 (http://jobs. aol.com/articles/2010/12/20/what-its-like-to-be-an-athletic-trainer-in-the-nfl-interview-w/).

Malinowski, Eric. "Illness, Injury Hit Hundreds of Olympic Athletes" *Wired.*, September 15, 2010. Retrieved August 2011(http://www.wired.com/playbook/2010/09/ olympic-illness-injury/).

McMahon, Patrick. *Current Diagnosis and Treatment in Sports Medicine.* New York, NY: McGraw-Hill Medical, 2006.

Micheli, Lyle J. *Sports Medicine Bible: Prevent, Detect, and Treat Your Sports Injuries Through the Latest Medical Techniques.* New York, NY: William Morrow, 1995.

Michigan State Athletic Training. "General Athletic Training Program Information." Retrieved August 2011 (http://athletictraining.msu.edu/prospective-students/ atgeneralinfo.html).

NATA. "About the NATA." Retrieved August 2011 (http:// www.nata.org/aboutNATA).

Quinn, Elizabeth. "Five Ways to Find a Job in Sports Medicine." About.com. Retrieved August 2011 (http:// sportsmedicine.about.com/od/educationemployment/ tp/Five-Ways-To-Find-A-Career-In-Sports-Medicine .htm).

Quinn, Elizabeth. "Top Search Engines for Sports Fitness Jobs." About.com. Retrieved August 2011

(http://sportsmedicine.about.com/od/
educationemployment/tp/Top-Search-Engines-For-
Sports-Fitness-Jobs.htm).

Rich, Brent S.E., and Mitchell K. Pratte. *Tarascon Sports
Medicine Pocketbook*. Sudbury, MA: Jones and Bartlett
Publishers, 2010.

Rink, Judith. *Teaching Physical Education for Learning*.
New York, NY: McGraw-Hill Humanities/Social
Sciences/Languages, 2009.

Rouzier, Pierre A. *The Sports Medicine Patient Advisor*.
Third edition. Amherst, MA: SportsMed Press, 2010.

Sewell, Dean, Philip Watkins, Murray Griffin, and Ken
Roberts. *Sport and Exercise Science: An Introduction*.
New York, NY: Edward Arnold Publishers, 2005.

SportsMindSkills.com. "The Rules of Sports Psychology."
Retrieved September 2011 (http://www.sportsmind-
skills.com/sports_psychology_rules.php).

Springen, Karen. "Sports Medicine Doctors Offer Tips
to Avoid and Treat Injuries." *Chicago Magazine*.
Retrieved September 2011 (http://www.chicagomag.
com/Chicago-Magazine/April-2011/Sports-Medicine-
Doctors-Offer-Tips-to-Avoid-and-Treat-Injuries/).

StateUniversity.com. "Physical Therapist Job Description,
Career as a Physical Therapist." Retrieved September
2011 (http://careers.stateuniversity.com/pages/489/
Physical-Therapist.html).

StateUniversity.com. "Sports Psychologist Job Description,
Career as a Sports Psychologist." Retrieved September
2011 (http://careers.stateuniversity.com/pages/7815/
Sports-Psychologist.html).

Sweet, Laurie. "How Is Ultrasound Used for Pain
Treatment During Physical Therapy?" ABC News.,
August 8, 2008. Retrieved September 2011 (http://abc-
news.go.com/Health/TreatingPain/story?id=4047863).

USA Today. "Social Anxiety Disorder: Miami Dolphin Ricky Williams." January 21, 2005. Retrieved September 2011 (http://www.usatoday.com/community/chat/2002-10-22-williams.htm).

Walker, Brad. *The Anatomy of Sports Injuries.* Berkeley, CA: North Atlantic Books, 2007.

Weinberg, Robert, and Daniel Gould. *Foundations of Sport and Exercise Psychology.* Champaign, IL: Human Kinetics, 2006.

INDEX

ABOUT THE AUTHOR

Laura La Bella is a lifelong runner who recently took up cycling and is mastering the art of kayaking. She is a writer who lives, works, paddles, and runs in and around Rochester, NY.

PHOTO CREDITS